THE GUIDIMAKA REGION OF MAURITANIA

THE GUIDIMAKA REGION OF MAURITANIA

A CRITICAL ANALYSIS LEADING TO A DEVELOPMENT PROJECT

Phillip Bradley
Claude Raynaut
Jorge Torrealba

A study sponsored by
WAR ON WANT (UK)
May 1977

Contents

Preface

This report is the outcome of the first stage in an undertaking which began about three years ago under the sponsorship of War on Want, a British non-governmental aid organisation. In November 1973, a public appeal was launched in Great Britain in response to the famine which struck the Sahelian countries and Ethiopia. A Sahel fund was thus established.

From the outset, War on Want did not take the view that this disaster was totally, or even essentially, induced by a climatic accident. Indeed, War on Want's analysis was that one could not assess the capacity of the Sahelian peoples to resist prolonged periods of drought without taking into account the profound social and economic changes which occurred over decades of colonial and neo-colonial domination.

From such a perspective, it followed that, in order to be effective, assistance could not be limited to emergency relief. Such action, while attacking immediate needs, was likely to heighten still more the dependence of the assisted populations. Instead, it was essential to tackle, as far as possible, the root causes of such dependencies. Thus the idea emerged of concentrating available financial resources on the implementation of an agricultural development project which, although limited in size, was likely to reinforce the overall production potential and improve the livelihood of a given population group.

The Guidimaka area was selected following a visit to Mauritania in June 1974 by War on Want's Sahel officer. Mauritania expressed the request that a non-governmental organisation finance an 'integrated' project within the Senegal river valley.

A preparatory mission designed to come forward with a diagnosis of the local situation and to gather the necessary elements for the formulation of a development project was decided on, and a research team was formed in November 1974. In order to cover a wide range of problems, this team included researchers from the three complementary fields of economic anthropology, agronomy and ecology.

Field studies were carried out on both the Senegalese and the Mauritanian sides of the Senegal river from March to May 1975. An overall report, together with proposals for a development project covering ten villages within the Département of Selibabi, were then submitted to the Mauritanian authorities. This report formed the basis on which an agreement was signed between the Government of Mauritania and War on Want on 28th February 1976.

The actual implementation of the development project began in June of the same year, and is planned to last for five years.

This paper is a revised version of the original report submitted to Mauritania in 1975; it has also been complemented by the addition of data collected during subsequent field studies in July 1976.

Some preliminary remarks are necessary in order to present the approach with which the original research study was conducted. Contrary to what is often done, we did not attempt to establish an exhaustive or systematic inventory of all the data relevant to the area studied. Such a method is only possible in the field when reliable data collected by the technical and administrative services are available, or when sufficient time and resources make it possible to organise oneself a systematic collection of data.

Neither was the case, and it was necessary for us to come quickly to an evaluation reliable enough to suggest the major orientations of an action programme. Thus a synthetic approach was adopted from the outset, whereby we considered the situation under study as a functional whole, whose interacting elements we would not be able to analyse in any great depth, but the diagnosis of which would highlight the most obvious manifestations of *disequilibrium*, as well as the positive factors of which it might be possible to take advantage.

This approach implies a 'short-cutting' of traditional scientific procedure, and that all observable data are not considered *a priori* as having the same importance. Instead, attention is focused on a limited number of factors which seem likely to have played a particular determining role in the evolution of the situation as a whole. Therefore, certain choices have to be made. These can only be effected on the basis of preliminary working hypotheses.

The primary hypothesis of our work was that in rural Africa a fundamental link exists between the way socio-economic systems function today and the forms of exploitation to which these systems were subject during the colonial period and to the present day. In the particular case of the Guidimaka, this led us to concentrate our thinking particularly on the emigration of active males, a long-established phenomenon of massive proportions, and to attempt to show its most significant consequences in terms of the social, economic and technical conditions of agricultural production.

A second hypothesis was that the effect of natural factors, and particularly of climatic vagaries, should not be underestimated, although they can in no way be regarded as ultimately determining; the impact of these factors combines in fact with that of more fundamental and lasting ones, of a socio-economic nature. It was therefore very important to go beyond a static description of the environment and to carry out a dynamic analysis of its evolution, taking into account the role of human factors and particularly of the emigration mentioned above.

Finally, a third hypothesis was that, in many cases, the most useful level for understanding the dynamics of the relationship between a group of farmers and their environment is that of the agricultural and land systems of the village. It is indeed at this level that negative and positive functional relationships are established between the potentialities of the environment, the social distribution of land and labour, and the orientation followed by the system of production under the pressure of the larger external economic forces. This is particularly true of the Guidimaka, where the settlement patterns show a distribution according to heavily populated agglomerations with deeply structured social communities.

Within this framework, our research objectives were defined as follows: To observe the disequilibria in the system of agricultural production, primarily at the level of the village social and spatial units, taking into account the role of natural factors, but with a special emphasis on the decisive role of socio-economic phenomena, in particular the specific form of colonial domination whose main feature is the development of emigration.

The method we followed enabled us to reconcile satisfactorily two contradictory requirements: on the one hand, the need for rigorous preliminary analysis and, on the other, the urgency of formulating an action-programme.

The outcome is undoubtedly schematic, but it has nevertheless made it possible to define a number of major orientations from which the agricultural development project presented in the section of this report has been formulated.

Many gaps need to be overcome, and a more in-depth analysis remains indispensable. It is necessary to come to a more precise understanding of each of the village communities, of the social and economic forces at work in these units, and their articulation within a system of environmental use. An in-depth study needs to be conducted not only at the level of family production units, their structure and their internal functioning, but also in terms of the forms of inequality and dependence which exist between these units within the same community.

One of the features of the project is the provision for the maintenance, throughout its implementation, of a research programme concerned with carrying out a continuous evaluation of the project operations, and with conducting the research necessary for achieving greater understanding of both the natural environment and socio-economic factors.

The original field research was carried out by P.N. Bradley (ecology), C. Raynaut (economic anthropology) and J. Torrealba (agronomy). However, from the outset in November 1974, the research team comprised five members, including C. Robbins (agronomy/sociology) and R. Elsner (co-ordinator for War on Want). During the field research, C. Raynaut acted as mission leader, and co-ordinated the writing up of the final report.

We wish to acknowledge the kindness of the following individuals, organisations and governments in offering their assistance and collaboration: The Government of the Islamic Republic of Mauritania, Jean-Francois Barres and the staff of IRAM (Paris), Messrs. Brunt and Varley of the Ministry of Agriculture, Fisheries and Food (UK), André Lericollais (ORSTOM), the CIDR team in Bakel, Michel Parsy, Iain MacDonald and Susan Phillips (War on Want), Abdoulaye Bathily, Phil O'Keefe, Fatima Bezzaz, and the staff of the Hotel Vichy, Dakar.

It should be noted that Parts I and II were written by the original research team comprising Claude Raynaut, Phillip Bradley and Jorge Torrealba, whereas Part III was written by the above and the other two members, Christopher Robbins and Richard Elsner.

PART I
Introduction

CHAPTER 1

The Guidimaka

The area of this study lies within the administrative region of the Guidimaka in the south-central area of the Islamic Republic of Mauritania. The Guidimaka itself extends to a northern limit of 15°56' and is marked in the south by the Senegal river: the political divide between Mauritania and Senegal. The eastern boundary is similarly delimited, by the Karakoro river: the frontier separating the Guidimaka and Mauritania from Mali. Finally, the western limits attain 12°44' W. This region therefore consists of an approximately rectangular land mass 140 km. by 100 km., with a surface area of 1000 sq. km.

Selibabi is the principal town of the Guidimaka, and supports a population of approximately 4000. It serves as both the regional administrative focus and the centre of one of the Guidimaka's three constituent départements. Within the département of Selibabi are three arrondissements, centring on Khabou, Gouraye, and Woumpou.

The physical setting of the Guidimaka is complex, not only in terms of its geology and relief, but also in its climatic and hydrological regimes, and in turn, its resultant ecology. The distinctive physical feature of the region is the Senegal river valley and its major tributaries: the Karakoro, Garfa, and the Niorde. The Senegal river flows from south-east to north-west across the southern margin of the Guidimaka. The Karakoro joins the Senegal at Khabou, the southern extremity of the region, flowing from the north and forming the region's eastern boundary. The two other tributaries drain the central and northern areas and flow into the Senegal river at Woumpou (Niorde) and Maghama (Garfa), the latter outside the administrative confines of the region. In addition to these major drainage systems, several minor valleys intersect the southern and central areas of the Guidimaka. Figure 1 shows the setting of the Guidimaka in its national context and Figure 2 illustrates the communications and settlements, and their administrative importance in the region.

The general topographic expression of these systems is one of alternating plains and minor relief features with the exception, however, of the Assaba massif in the north. This plateau, bounded by steep escarpments, rises to a height of 200-300 m. and extends northwards from the centre of the Guidimaka to the semi-desert

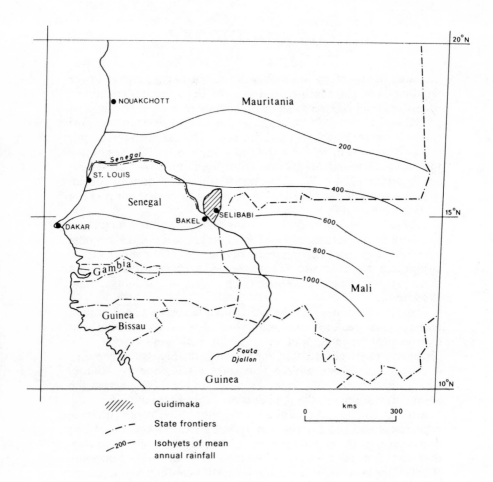

NOUAKCHOTT

Mauritania

200

Senegal
ST. LOUIS

400

Senegal

15°N

BAKEL SELIBABI

600

DAKAR

800

Gambia

1000

Mali

Guinea
Bissau

Fouta
Djallon

Guinea

10°N

20°N

/////. Guidimaka

—·— State frontiers

—200— Isohyets of mean
annual rainfall

kms

0   300

Fig. 1 Guidimaka and its national setting

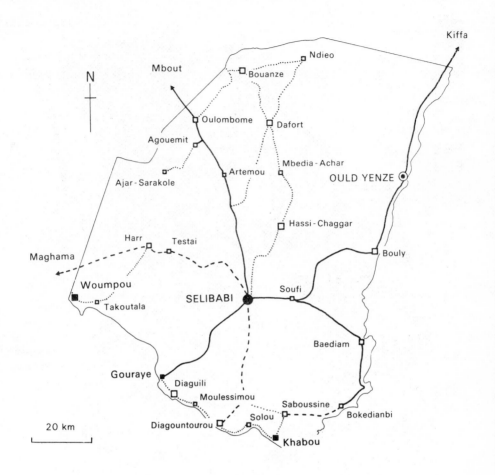

Fig. 2 Guidimaka: settlements and communications

administrative centres:–

● of region and département

◉ of département

■ of arrondissement

□ ▫ other settlements

principal routes
— permanently practicable
– – intermittently practicable

secondary routes
⋯ intermittently practicable

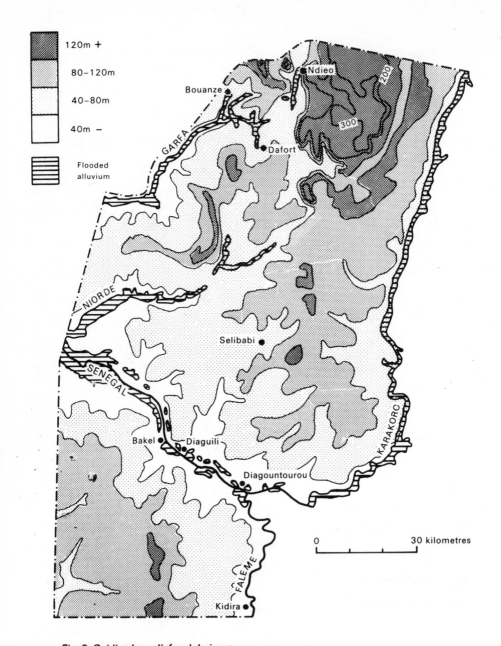

Fig. 3 Guidimaka: relief and drainage

120m +

80–120m

40–80m

40m –

Flooded
alluvium

Ndieo

Bouanze

GARFA

Dafort

200

300

NIORDE

SENEGAL

Selibabi

Bakel

Diaguili

Diagountourou

KARAKORO

0   30 kilometres

FALEME

Kidira

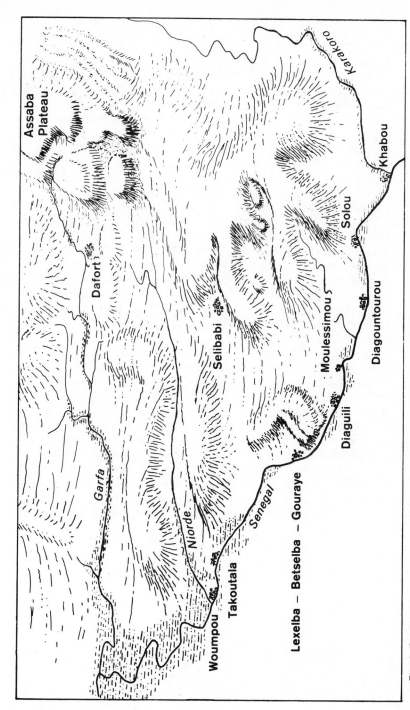

Fig. 4 Guidimaka: sketch diagram illustrating relief, drainage, and selected settlements

regions north-west of Kiffa. Apart from this major relief block, the topography is characterised by gently rising dissected uplands surmounted by inselbergs and quartzite ridges. The alluvial areas vary in extent, those close to the Senegal river being much wider than those of the interior tributaries. Thus the floodlands in the region of Woumpou may attain 5 km. in width, whilst those close to Ndieo in the far north rarely extend for more than 0.5 km. A similar gradient is noticeable along the Senegal valley itself, the alluvium of Khabou being considerably less extensive than that of Woumpou. A visual impression of the relief and drainage of the Guidimaka can be gained from Figures 3 and 4.

Climatically, the Guidimaka lies in the southern transition zone between the Sahel to the north and the Sudan to the south. The semi-arid state of this area results from a predominantly dry climate, punctuated by a three-month rainy season between July and September. Mean annual rainfall at Selibabi is 616 mm., falling to approximately 450 mm. in the north and increasing to as much as 660 mm. in the extreme south. However, as with all semi-arid monsoonal climates, significant variations occur between years and locations.

The soils and vegetation of the Guidimaka are controlled essentially by its climate, although the alluvial lands bordering the Senegal river support a series of distinctive vegetation types primarily influenced by the soil and its hydrological regime. The prevailing vegetation of the region as a whole reflects the influence of a transitional climate. A clear gradient is observable in the change from open shrub savanna in the north to a more densely wooded Sudan savanna in the south. Local variation is determined by soils and water supply, and this is nowhere more evident than in the Senegal valley alluvium, where a complex pattern of levees, terraces and depressions gives rise to a markedly differentiated series of soils and an intricate sequence of vegetation associations.

CHAPTER 2

Climate and Hydrology

I CLIMATE

1. Seasonal Rhythms

The Guidimaka region lies within the Sahelian zone of West Africa, more specifically the Sahel-Sudan transition sector (Trochain, 1940). Rainfall is initiated by the northwards progression of the Intertropical Convergence Zone (ITCZ), a latitudinal belt of surface disturbance separating a humid maritime air mass to the south-west and a hotter, more arid system of the Saharan interior. This zone of frontal activity intrudes progressively further inland as the maritime air mass is drawn in behind the northwards progression of the sun. A lag effect is evident in this seasonal rhythm. The sun reaches its equinox in mid-June, but the ITCZ only attains its northerly maximum in mid-August. The surface discontinuity migrates well into the desert to a latitude of 20-22°N, while the Guidimaka lies between 14°40'N and 15°56'N. Thus the ITCZ passes northwards over the southern Guidimaka in mid-May and returns in late September. Because of the shallow slope of the front, rain-bearing clouds are unable to evolve close to its ground surface junction and only develop sufficient vertical extension some 400 km. behind. It is for this reason that the rainy season does not commence until late June/early July, a month after the surface disturbance has normally passed to the north.

The precise position of the ITCZ at any given time, and its rate of migration, vary not only from year to year, but also over a much shorter time period. Daily movements of as much as 200 km. have been recorded in central Mali by Garnier (1967), although the proximity of the coast to the Guidimaka would tend to damp down such gross oscillations. These characteristics of the ITCZ are doubtless partly responsible for both annual and short-term irregularities in the precipitation of the region. As a consequence, the resultant mean annual rainfall totals and coefficients of variability of 616 mm. and 25.2 per cent for Selibabi and 508 mm. and 23.4 per cent for Bakel are by no means atypical of this West African latitudinal belt. In fact, similar data from other stations within the 14° to 16°N latitudinal zone of Senegal, Mauritania and Mali suggest the coefficient of variation of nearer 30 per cent is more usual. It seems that the Guidimaka occupies a position between the more extreme continental oscillations of the ITCZ to the east, and the counteracting influence of coastal wind disturbances of western Senegal. This relative stability is in fact revealed in the account of drought intensity given below.

Throughout the rest of the year, a predictable pattern of climatic changes is observable. Following the end of the rains, in late September/early October, humid conditions prevail until the end of the year. Throughout this period, changeable wind conditions gradually give way to a steady north-easterly air stream emanating from the central Sahara. This dust-laden and dessicating wind, akin to the harmattan of northern Nigeria and Niger, builds in strength as the maritime air beneath the ITCZ moves further and further to the south. From late November until the following March this wind persists at varying intensities. When not dust-laden, clear skies predominate, with resultant loss of heat during the night. Diurnal temperature ranges increase from a minimum of 6°C in August to upwards of 17°C in January and February. At the same time, evapotranspiration increases to twice that of the rainy season. Commensurate decreases in relative humidity occur, falling from a maximum in August, September and October of over 90 per cent to a March and April minimum of 12 per cent. Selected meteorological statistics are shown in Appendix B(i).

By the end of March, north-easterly winds decline in vigour, and a relatively calm period heralds the return of the ITCZ. Mean monthly temperatures increase from 24°C in January to 35°C in May, relative humidity rises towards the rainy season maximum while, because of the high temperatures and reduced diurnal range, evaporation reaches its annual maximum four times that experienced during the height of the rainy season. This pre-rain season is the least comfortable from the human viewpoint, being extremely hot and humid with minimal night-time cooling. By mid-June a perceptible change is observable, as cloud amounts increase and temperatures decline, albeit undramatically. This weather pattern finally breaks as the first storms indicate the passage of the front and the arrival of the rains.

With minor variations according to location, this seasonal pattern is characteristic, not only of the Guidimaka, but throughout semi-arid West Africa. In relating climatic patterns to agriculture, acknowedgment of such local variations, and indeed of the whole question of rainfall effectiveness, is of fundamental importance.

2. Rainfall Effectiveness

The concept of the effectiveness or the utility of rainfall is a complex one which is not readily amenable to rapid analysis or explanation. In the Guidimaka region only one weather station exists, at Selibabi, and for the river areas the nearest recording station is at Bakel on the Senegalese bank. With information limited to these two sources, only general statements can be made. In this section, questions rather than answers are offered; questions which raise some of the important issues relating to rainfall effectiveness from the viewpoint of agriculture.

(a) *The utility of annual rainfall returns*

Although annual and monthly returns are available from local stations, and illustrate the basic climatic pattern of the area, the use of such data for forecasting agricultural production or, indeed, for explaining past events is, of course, severely limited. Several problems of interpretation are immediately apparent:

(i) *Winter rains.* The Guidimaka falls within the West African rainfall zone which receives rain not only from the ITCZ during the summer months, but also from occasional cyclones which pass to the south of the Mediterranean during the winter months. Although rare, and contributing only a small proportion of annual totals, these freak rain events undermine the value of long-term analysis based on available annual totals.

(ii) *Intensity and regularity.* Agriculture is affected as much by short-term variation of rainfall as by total quantity (Bradley, 1973). Both the intensity and the regularity of rainstorms are of critical importance to crops, and yet are not revealed in the more easily available published accounts.

(iii) *Infiltration and run-off.* The effectiveness of rain in supporting plant growth is in part a function of infiltration and run-off. As a general rule the more intense the rainfall, the greater will be the loss through run-off (Delwaulle, 1973; Kowal, 1970). Kowal's work in Nigeria suggests that fifty per cent or more may be lost through overland flow. In many of the alluvial soils of the Senegal valley, high clay and silt percentages prevent rapid infiltration. Much of the total rainfall is thus lost and unavailable to crops. Soil water-retention capacity will affect growth of crops both during the wet season and in the dry season if irrigation is practised. Provided saturation is reached during the wet season, clay soils have greater storage capacity, although their wilting point is higher. Moreover, the study by the Mission d'Aménagement du Fleuve Sénégal (MAS) (Sogetha, 1962, P21) suggests that despite inundation by floods of the lowest alluvium, only the top layer of these clay-rich soils may become fully saturated.

(iv) *Evaporation*. One of the key factors in assessing the effectiveness of rainfall is, of course, evaporation. Notwithstanding the difficulties of interpreting the wide range of evaporation estimates available, the physical problems of providing base information from which to calculate these estimates must also be considered. The simplest estimate, derived from Thornthwaite and Mather (1957), requires only monthly temperature readings and can therefore be applied to the Guidimaka. However, this estimate of potential evapotranspiration lacks sufficient precision and accuracy to be interpreted in terms of water need for crops. More sophisticated estimates of actual evaporation have been derived by Bowen (1926) and Penman (1948) and others, but in all cases currently unavailable information such as vapour pressure gradients, insolation and wind speed are required. Finally, direct measurements of potential evaporation can be made from open pans. All of these methods have limitations, and the range of values shown in Appendix B(i) gives evidence of the difficulties such figures pose when attempting to apply evaporation measurements to agricultural forecasting. At this stage only general statements can be made with regard to evaporation losses in the Guidimaka.

In the rainy season, the irregular intervals between rainstorms and the varying intensity and quantity of the rain itself imply alternating water surplus and water deficiency. Even though evaporation estimates on a monthly basis suggest a lessening problem during the humid months, there undoubtedly occur periods of dessication during the growing season. This is particularly evident at the start of the rains in June and July, when it is not unusual for seedlings to die because of moisture stress over a short period (Bradley, 1973). A second consideration lies in the much greater potential evaporation losses in the latter half of the dry season. The assessment of irrigation requirements at this time is more directly concerned with evaporation because of the possibility of regulated rather than unpredictable water inputs.

(v) *Spatial variation*. A final point pertaining to the utility of rainfall statistics and the establishment of effectiveness is the problem of relating point-based data to what is, in fact, a spatially continuous phenomenon. Rain does not fall on to one specific location, but over an area within which the volume of water is not distributed isotropically. There is no doubt that rainfall varies over short distances in the Sahel and that this variation can be extreme. Thus, for planning purposes, the use of data from Bakel as a substitute for Diaguili (9 km. to the south-east) is questionable beyond an approximation. The difference in annual totals between Bakel and Selibabi is 108 mm. over 40 km., the latter receiving the greater amount despite being 28 km. further north. By contrast, Kidira, 60 km. south-east of Bakel, receives an annual total which is 224 mm. greater than the latter. Although the annual climatic rhythm is consistent in a general sense, detailed spatial patterns do not necessarily relate directly to the north-south movement of the ITCZ.

Even greater differences occur with monthly figures over shorter distances. Thus, at Bakel two recording stations — one in the town, and one 7 km. to the south at the airfield — reveal a range of variation over the years 1955-65 of + 26 per cent to -47 per cent. Translated into absolute quantities, Bakel airfield received 689 mm. in 1959 as against 562 mm. in Bakel town, and 235 mm. in 1958 compared to 441 mm. Full tables for the ten years are shown in Appendix B(ii). In attempting to relate cropping patterns to climatic conditions for the ten villages under review, it is important to note that Woumpou is 48 km. further north than Khabou. Despite their joint location within the Sahel-Sudan transition zone, the two villages, and indeed those in between, do not share a common rainfall total. Finally, it should be realised that the variations over short distances for any one year, as exemplified at Bakel, are often in excess of the range of annual deviations witnessed during the drought years between 1968 and 1973.

3. The Drought

Although the most extreme effects of the 1968-73 drought were felt further north than the Guidimaka, the region itself suffered severe rainfall deficits during that period. It should be remembered, however, that drought-induced disasters are recurrent themes of such climatically marginal environments and the most recent example, despite its extreme nature, should be seen in the context of an agricultural economy adapted to periodic rainfall deficiency.

During the drought years, the area suffered a gross annual rainfall deficit of approximately 25 per cent. It should be appreciated, however, that this general figure obscures both spatial and temporal variations, as emphasised in the previous section. Thus, in 1971 Selibabi received ten per cent less than mean annual rainfall, while Kiffa, 150 km. to the north and just outside the

Guidimaka, sustained a 52 per cent shortfall. Similar differences occur from year to year, with 1958, 1972 and 1973 being the worst years. Detailed figures of annual totals measured at a number of rainfall stations in the region and immediately surrounding it are shown in Table I.

There is no doubt that the drought caused a severe upset in the prevailing agricultural pattern and the general social conditions of the region. Evidence of the effect of the drought can be seen in the near exhaustion of grain reserves in many of the villages and the adoption of such new crops as *nabane*, a variety of sorghum previously found further north and demonstrably more resistant to drier conditions. Despite these changes and other evidence of drought impact illustrated below, it is important not to over-emphasise the role of the drought in creating the changing conditions of local society. Relating a 25 per cent rainfall deficit to crop performance or, indeed, to any other factor of social and economic life, is a difficult problem. Precipitation statistics are not a reliable guide to the impact of such climatic phenomena upon society. The local resource base for agriculture is obviously primarily affected by climatic vicissitudes, but rainfall itself is only one determinant of the potential agricultural capacity of the region. The realisation of the potential is dependent upon a number of other factors, particularly social and economic, which may assume a greater importance than rainfall itself in any given situation. As will be seen in later chapters, the importance of these factors is equal to or greater than that of the physical deficiency of the primary resource of agriculture.

In addition to its obvious impact on agricultural potential, the drought should also be seen in terms of the regional environmental resource base. Climate itself is but one of a series of physical factors which determine the potential of the area. Local geology and topography, local soils and vegetation are all influential in determining the possibilities of the river areas. The impact of the drought on such physical factors as vegetation and soils will also be important in determining future possibilities. These aspects are covered in later chapters of the report.

II. HYDROLOGY AND THE ANNUAL FLOOD

Towards the end of the dry season the flow of the Senegal river declines to little more than a trickle. The bank, the alluvial land behind, and the flood cycle of the river are important components of the region's agricultural production system.

Table I
Rainfall characteristics of the southern Guidimaka

	Matam	Selibabi	Bakel	Kidira	Kayes
mean (mm)	508	616	508	732	715
standard error (mm)	25	26	17	34	23
standard deviation (mm)	172	155	119	208	184
coefficient of variation (%)	34	25	23	29	23
rainfall (mm)					
1968	286	414	484	386	480
1969	534	510	575	762	798
1970	281	388	457	598	556
1971	431	554	541	552	596
1972	175	606	369	623	485
1973	220	444	395	410	559
percentage deviation from mean					
1968	−44	−33	−6	−47	−33
1969	+5	−17	+13	+4	+12
1970	−45	−37	−10	−18	−22
1971	−15	−10	+6	−25	−17
1972	−66	−2	−27	−15	−32
1973	−57	−28	−22	−44	−22
standard scores					
1968	−1.3	−1.3	−0.2	−1.7	−1.3
1969	+0.2	−0.7	+0.6	+0.1	+0.5
1970	−1.3	−1.5	−0.4	−0.6	−0.9
1971	−0.4	−0.4	+0.3	−0.9	−0.6
1972	−1.9	−0.1	−1.2	−0.5	−1.2
1973	−1.7	−1.1	−1.0	−1.5	−0.8

probability (number of years in 100 at or below which the rainfall totals experienced during the years 1968-73 can be expected)

	Matam	Selibabi	Bakel	Kidira	Kayes
1968	10	10	42	5	10
1969	56	25	71	56	67
1970	9	7	33	26	19
1971	33	34	61	19	26
1972	3	48	12	30	11
1973	5	13	17	6	20

The major catchment area of the Senegal river lies far to the south of the Guidimaka in the Fouta Djallon highlands. During its annual progression north and then south, the ITCZ passes across the Fouta Djallon several weeks before it arrives in the Guidimaka region itself. Thus, rainfall starts in the catchment area of the Senegal river before it arrives further north in the Guidimaka. The flow rate of the Senegal river is such that the resultant recharge of water does not in fact reach the Guidimaka until after the rains have begun in early July. By mid-August, however, the discharge is such that the height of the river has increased to the extent that the difference between water surface and bank top falls to five metres or less. As the height of the river increases and reaches this level, water flows through the tributary channels which breach the bank, into the lower alluvial lands behind. It is at this time that the major flood of the alluvial lands begins. The mean date, based on sixty years of records, is 16th August. The Mission d'Amenagement du Fleuve Sénégal (MAS) (1960) suggest that penetration of flood-waters through these breached levees into the alluvial lands starts when a continuous discharge of 2,000 cubic metres per second is attained. By mid-August such a discharge occurs and active flooding then begins, lasting until approximately 3rd October, when the height and discharge rate of the river declines below the 2,000 cubic metres-per-second threshold. The difference in height of the water surface in the river between its minimum in the dry season and its maximum at the peak of flooding can be as much as 12 m. Thus, the flooding pattern of the Senegal river and the fact that its headwaters lie further south in highland regions, receiving earlier and more plentiful rainfall, liken it to those other major rivers flowing northward through semi-arid Africa, such as the Niger and the Nile.

The lag effect evident between the onset of the rains and the initiation of this major annual flood is important to the agriculture of the region. The rains themselves start towards the end of June or early July, and yet extensive inundation does not begin until mid-August. However, in this interim period the rainfall itself may cause localised, unpredictable flooding of short duration. This unpredictability means that agricultural activities in the lower alluvium are in a state of flux until the more consistent flooding pattern commences in mid-August. As far as the major flood is concerned, its duration and effectiveness are determined by annual vagaries in total rainfall. Using 2000 cubic metres per second as a threshold figure, Appendix C shows the period of active flooding at Bakel from 1904 to 1964.

The range of values demonstrated by these figures — 85 days in

1924, to a minimum of none in 1913, 1914, 1944 and much more recently in 1974 suggests that, although the annual pattern of flooding is consistent from year to year and predictable in terms of the agricultural calendar, the height of flooding and, following this, the area of land inundated for sufficient time to enable cropping cycles to be completed, are extremely variable. The standard deviation is, in fact, 21 days, with a coefficient of variation of 43 per cent. In terms of probabilities, this means that in six years out of ten the most precise statement that can be made about the duration of flooding is only that it will be between 28 and 70 days. With such a high coefficient of variability a narrow range of flooding duration, such as between 45 and 55 days, can only be predicted in two years out of ten. Therefore, whereas the annual flood and the annual rainy season are regular and expected events, their intensity and duration are highly variable. It would be wrong to assume that, because this particular agricultural region receives its water via two regular annual events, problems of water supply to crops do not occur. Despite these two annual events, the agricultural potential of the Guidimaka is very much affected by the variability of water supply.

The same problem that existed in relating rainfall figures to agricultural effectiveness exists with the annual flood. Although it is possible to predict within certain limits the duration of active flooding, this does not tell us the degree to which farming activities can be programmed to maximise efficient use of the water supply. In particular, the relationship between the duration and height of flooding, and the areal extent of the alluvial lands which are inundated, is not known with any certainty. Because of the importance of flood-retreat agriculture during the latter half of the rainy season and the ensuing dry season, the acquisition of this knowledge is of paramount importance. MAS (1960) have general estimates of the total alluvial land downstream of Bakel for the Senegalese side of the river, and of the area inundated by weak, medium and strong floods. These are illustrated in Table II.

Table II
Areas of flooded land of the Senegal valley below Bakel

Total alluvial land below Bakel	800,000 hectares
Weak flood (1944), area inundated	100,000 hectares (12.5%)
Medium flood (1953), area inundated	370,000 hectares (46.3%)
Strong flood (1954), area inundated	500,000 hectares (52.5%)

No such figures are available for the riverlands of the Guidimaka. However, calculations of total alluvial land and the proportion occupied by the lowest areas liable to sustain extensive and long duration flooding have been completed from maps and air photographs and are summarised in Table III.

Table III
Alluvial land of the southern Guidimaka and the Bakel region

	Senegal, Dembankane to Ballou	Mauritania, Woumpou to Khabou
a) Total alluvial land	143.4 sq.km.	159.9 sq.km.
b) Lowest areas liable to flooding	51.3 sq. km	41.5 sq. km.
c) As percentage of (a)	35.8%	26.0%

The extent of this land which is inundated by weak, medium and strong floods is not known. A more detailed analysis of the alluvial land which is flooded in the environs of the villages between Woumpou and Khabou is shown in Table IV.

Table IV
Alluvial lands of the Senegal river villages of the Guidimaka

	Total alluvial land (sq.km.)	Lowest areas regularly flooded (sq.km.)
Woumpou & Takoutala	53.4	12.6 (23.6%)
Gouraye, Betselba & Lexelba	15.5	5.7 (36.8%)
Diaguili	28.4	3.4 (12.1%)
Moulessimou & Diogountourou	22.9	5.9 (25.8%)
Solou & Khabou	39.8	14.0 (35.2%)

Although these estimates are of necessity crude, they nevertheless give some indication of the overall availability of the different types of land to the different villages. One interesting point from this Table is the resource base of Diaguili, the largest village along the river front. Although containing a median amount of alluvial land, very little is flooded with any regularity. This point is in fact manifest in the degree to which Diaguili, more than any other village of the Guidimakan riverine areas, depends to a greater extent on its interior, drier lands for food production.

CHAPTER 3

Geology and Topography

The geological foundation of the Guidimaka and its surrounding region is represented by rocks which span the whole of geological history, from the Precambrian to the Holocene. Ancient intrusive and metamorphic rocks occur as isolated hills and ridges, sedimentary strata provide the basis for extensive plateaux, and superficial alluvial deposits are widespread. Appendices D and E give a geological map of the area and a detailed chronological history of the quaternary.

Four basic topographic units can be identified, commencing from that part of Senegal south-west of Bakel and extending northwards and slightly eastwards to the north border of the Guidimaka.

The first of these regions consists of an elevated plateau 50-100m. above the Senegal valley floor to the north-east. This plateau has for its foundation the tertiary sediments of the Continental Terminal, and gives rise to a gently undulating surface surmounted by a near-continuous sheet of lateritic cuirass. This cuirass has evolved from the parent sandstones laid down in the mid to late tertiary period. It is broken by a series of south-west flowing drainage systems which are manifest in shallow valleys, occasionally bounded by abrupt escarpments maintained by the durability of the lateritic cuirass. This plateau dips to the west and rises to its extreme point on its north-eastern margin, whereupon it abruptly descends to the alluvial plain of the Senegal valley.

The Senegal valley plain forms the second major unit of the region and may vary in width from 5 to 10 km. in the north-west to only 1 km. in the extreme south-east. It consists of a series of variably aged alluvial deposits, all quaternary, described in more detail below, and comprises the fundamental agricultural resource of those villages bordering the Senegal river.

On the north-eastern, Mauritanian side of the river, beyond this alluvium, lies a series of undulating hills and plains founded upon more ancient crystalline and metamorphic rocks. These hills comprise the third unit. Their foundation may be of acidic rocks such as granites and quartzites, or of more basaltic material, giving rise to richer weathering products. The relief based upon these geological features is variable. In some cases long linear quartzite ridges are dominant features of the landscape, in others isolated granite inselbergs can be seen. In addition, there exist upland features which extend for several tens of kilometres, presenting a rolling upland topography. The details of these various rocks are given in Appendix D. From the viewpoint of agricultural resources, the important factor relating to this geology is the way in which it has been dissected and in which there now exist extensive and well-integrated fluvial systems. These systems can be likened in some respects to the Senegal river itself, in that they have developed both alluvium and colluvium, based upon the surrounding hills. The extent of these deposits is variable; in the interior they are little more than minor depressions and narrow terraces, but where these systems debauch into the alluvium of the Senegal valley itself they may become quite extensive and present viable agricultural areas. The quality of soils associated not only with the uplands themselves but with their associated alluvium is to a certain extent dependent on the basic geology of the uplands. Where basaltic rocks appear on the surface, richer soils can be found. By contrast, in the more acidic, granitic areas less fertile soils have evolved.

The fourth topographic and geologic region is that of the Assaba massif to the north of the central Guidimaka. This feature extends as an elevated plateau from an area some 40 km. north of Selibabi as far as the desert margins north-west of Kiffa, and is based upon Silurian and Ordovician sandstones, horizontally bedded and giving rise to an elevated plateau. It is bounded by steep escarpments, except on its eastern margin, where remnants of a fossil sand-dune system abut the plateau and disguise its margins. Figure 4 illustrates the basic topography of this region. In association with Figure 3, a basic relief presentation is offered.

Although the solid geology determines the basic parameters of relief within the area, much of it is obscured by more recent deposits, which are in fact of greater importance to the agriculture of the Guidimaka. The alluvial sediments, not only of the Senegal river itself, but also of its northern-based tributaries, have already been mentioned and will be discussed in more detail below. In addition to this, surface materials throughout much of the Guidimaka overlie its solid foundation. Thus, a number of sand-dune systems are found, in particular, remnants of the fossil dunefield of the early quaternary, 'les dunes rouges'; just as on the Continental Terminal in Senegal some of the interior intermontane basins have developed lateritic surfaces, some of which are massive and covered with a thin sand veneer. Alternatively, they may have been eroded and redeposited to form a superficial layer of lateritic gravel. The borders of the interior drainage systems are generally covered by a variable thickness of colluvium, again of importance to the agriculture. The properties and benefits of some of these surface materials are discussed in more detail in Chapter 4 relating to soils and vegetation.

It has already been stated that a full chronological history of the quaternary deposits of the Senegal valley is given in Appendix E. However, before embarking on an analysis of the soil potential of the region, a brief account of these alluvial deposits is given. Three basic forms exist: the river bank itself, termed the *falo*, the top of the river bank, which is in fact an elevated levee standing above even the highest floods, and is called the *fonde*, and finally those depressions which lie to the rear of the *fonde* away from the river itself. These depressions, termed the *walo*, are flooded annually and are entirely different in character from the levees themselves. The nomenclature of these three major divisions and of the subdivisions which exist within them is common to the whole of the Senegal valley below Bakel and is used particularly in the context of those areas downstream of Matam. They are Toucouleur in origin, and although used in the areas of the Guidimaka, are generally supplanted by a more subtle and local classification. This is described in Chapter 4.

CHAPTER 4

Soils and Vegetation

I THE SOILS

The formation of soil and the development of its resultant properties, particularly with respect to agricultural potential, is a function of several factors. In the context of the Guidimaka the influence of geology, hydrology and time are of particular importance. The geological basis of soil formation in the region has already been described and is particularly important in the context of basaltic or acidic base geology and the influence of such features as the more recent lateritic development. The hydrological control is related to the annual pattern of rainfall and the flooding regime of the Senegal river and its tributaries. Not only does this annual water cycle lead to alternate wetting and drying of soils, but the flooding pattern of the river gives rise to long periods of inundation, and in certain circumstances permanent hydromorphic activity. Thus, the influence of water may be seen in terms of annually repeated events and permanently humid or, in other cases, arid conditions. The third factor of soil development, that of time, is best seen in the development of alluvium in both the Senegal valley and its tributaries. Soil processes in these deposits are primarily a function of time, given that water conditions within the soils are a function of the topography previously outlined. Some of these deposits are so recent that little profile development has taken place, and variations from site to site along them may be so great as to prevent any overall characterisation of quality. This is particularly true of the high *fonde* areas which are most recent in origin. As an alternative we may look at the *walo* areas, which are older in development and retain consistent properties, particularly with respect to the cycle of sedimentation and the development of soil profiles. Appendix E outlines the main sequence of quarternary events which has led to the peculiar configuration of the alluvial deposits and gives a better understanding of the relative rates of development of the major soil types of the alluvium.

We shall present our analysis of the soils of the region according to two perspectives: Firstly we shall describe the classification established by local farmers in terms of the properties of these soils and the use to which they are put. Secondly, we shall present some data concerning the physical and chemical properties of the soil

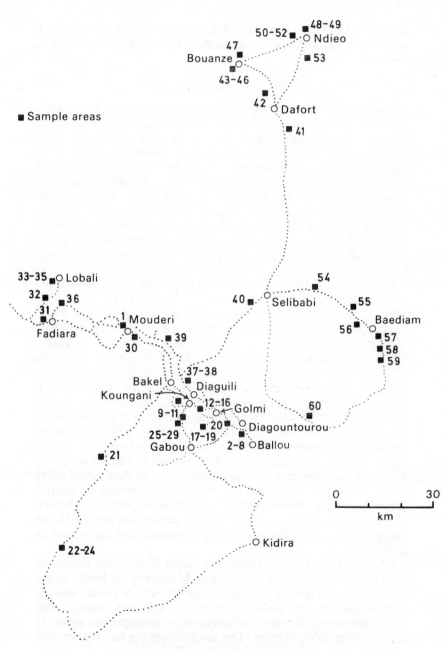

■ Sample areas

Fig. 5 Guidimaka and the neighbouring areas of Senegal:
sample sites and route of the soil and vegetation survey

samples taken in the spring of 1975. A map showing the sites from which both soil and vegetation samples were collected is shown in Figure 5.

1. *Traditional Classification of Soils*

It is apparent from our investigations in the region that the farmers of the Guidmaka are very well aware of the different potential of the soils of the region and their relation with topography. This differentiation of resources is subtle and complex, both in its realisation of the topographical controls of resource potential, and in its acknowledgment of the properties of the soils themselves. Thus we find two types of classification relating to land and soil. The system based on topography acknowledges the primary division of the drier upland *dieri* and the lower, more humid, alluvial areas. Within this, a series of minor subdivisions is noted.

Because of its physical properties the *dieri* understandably offers a restricted range of agricultural resource potential. By their nature the lateritic soils and soil pockets within the rocky upland areas are of little use to agriculture. The only terrain forms which are relevant to farming are the sand-dunes, or those pediplains which have accumulated a sufficient depth of superficial material. Where sand dunes exist in an extensive form they are known as *guillu*. Otherwise, specific names seem to be absent. In general, the whole of this terrain is termed the *dieri*. However, within this rather general recognition there exist special areas which are of greater importance. Thus, drainage systems and their associated patterns of alluvium and colluvium are specifically recognised and known as the *paraole* and the *rakhe*. The former relates to those slopes which lead down to the lowest and flattest alluvial areas bordering interior valley systems. The latter, the *rakhe*, pertain to the lowest areas, which may be likened to the major depressions of the Senegal valley itself. These two terms are not necessarily confined to interior drainage systems. Where such systems integrate with the alluvium of the Senegal river, or where certain conditions prevail in the Senegal valley itself, the terminology of *paraole* and *rakhe* may be applied.

Regarding the riverine lands, the major distinctions drawn by local farmers, as we noted in Chapter 3, concern the banks of the river or *falo*, the levee at the top of the river bank or *fonde*, and the depressions or the *walo*. Despite its apparent clarity, this classification can become confusing when attempts are made to apply it to specific instances. This results from the fact that criteria of topography and those related to soil qualities are frequently intermixed. Thus, it is sometimes difficult to obtain from farmers a clear distinction between *falo* and *fonde*, or frequently between *falo* and *walo*.[1] Often, alluvial lands are equally called *falo* or *walo*, the dominant criteria being the very similar qualities of both soils. However, it should be noted that this confusion may well have been enhanced by our use of informants originating from settlements on Karakoro, where the distinction between *falo* and *walo* is inapplicable.

Those areas of the *walo* that provide a suitable farming environment are termed *collengal*. This term relates more to their use as farming lands than to their position with respect to flooding or to their specific soil properties. A *collengal* is an area of *walo* which is recognised as valuable farming land. Some subdivisions of the *falo/fonde* areas are also recognised, but again with perhaps less emphasis than that which relates to soil property. On inside bends of meanders a sandbank is often present and this is termed a *fare*, a name which also applies to certain raised, bank-like features which may occur on the *falo* or on the *fonde* itself. The *falo* may be divided into two components, the *wuso*, a lower level of gentle gradient which may be farmed during the dry season by irrigation, and a higher, steeper slope termed the *falo*. Within the *fonde* a series of ridges may be present, depending on the particular local alluvial history. Between these ridges there often exist small shallow depressions called *napo*, which are very minor topographical features, but nevertheless have different soil properties and are therefore considered an important but different component of the *fonde* system. These depressions receive water not via an integrated drainage system, but more by surface runoff over a wide area. Where more expansive, and containing lakes for a considerable period during the dry season, such depressions, or rather the lakes they contain, are termed *khare*. In addition to surface runoff, they may be fed by clearly formed channel systems.

A second classificatory system of greater importance is that of the soil properties themselves. This system, for example, recognises the greater divergence of types within the *dieri*, as well as properties relating to the alluvium. In the *dieri*, for example, sand-dune areas are generally termed *signa*, but the *signa* may consist of three separate types. Thus, there is the *signa khole*, consisting of light-coloured sandy deposits, primarily used for the cultivation of groundnuts. The second type of sand, the *signa bine*, is darker in colour, slightly heavier, and of slightly greater fertility, although again it is used primarily for groundnut cultivation. A third type, the *signa kape*, relates to quite specific areas, in which the sand systems of the *dieri* abut on to the alluvium of the *walo*, such that a thin, sandy layer may overlie a basic, clay-rich sediment. These areas are more fertile, in that the soil base is more variable and often contains higher proportions of silt and clay. Away from the sand-dune areas, particularly in the pediplains, is a soil type which is sandy in nature but nevertheless contains proportions of fine elements and is known as the *niarwalle*. This leads in a sequential fashion to a more clay-rich soil, the *katamagne*, a term which pertains not only to the better areas of the interior, but also to the heavier, clay soils of the alluvium. Within the *niarwalle* are small depressions called the *niarikata*, which contain a mixture of both sand and clay. Although generally limited in extent, they offer good possibilities for agriculture. We find again a lesser precision of classification in relation to the alluvial lands. In the same way that divisions between *falo* and *fonde* and *walo* were not always clear, similarly, those between the soil types are generally referred to as *katamagne*. Subtle differences between the silty and sandy soils of the *fonde* and the heavier clayey soils of the *walo* are not readily apparent in the local typology. It is possible that further studies will reveal a finer classification of these areas. In the meantime, it appears that those agricultural lands close to settlements are recognised as much by their individual names, denoting ownership, proprietary use or location, as by any soil or topographic criteria. Thus, at Diaguili there exist such farmlands as the *budampu collengal*, the *worokhomo signa* and the *khirin kare*. These prefixes refer to the location of the particular field and are known not only by such locational terms but by their general properties in relation to agriculture. It is possible that at a later date a more precise and subtle definition of these individual areas may be specified.

The major components of these land systems are illustrated in Figure 6, where both soil and topographic classifications are included.

2. *Soil properties*

A series of soil samples was taken in both the alluvial lands and the *dieri*, and technical details of their qualities are offered in Appendix IV, 1a and b. The classification of these soils is based largely on the topographical definition which is more general to the Senegal valley as a whole, and not on the localised scheme of the Guidimaka. These soils show the following general properties:
1. The lowest parts of the basin may contain permanent lakes or *khare*. The soils of these areas are dominated by clay (50% +) and are in a condition of permanent reduction, due to submergence in excess of 150 days. These are not farmed because of the

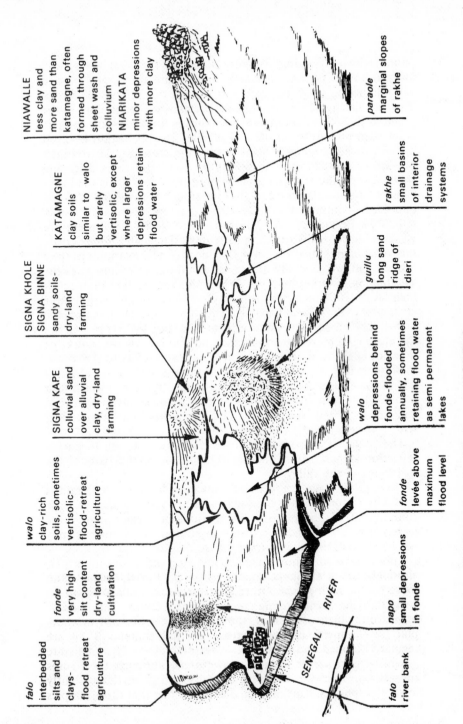

Fig. 6 Sketch diagram illustrating the major soil and land systems of Guidimaka

falo interbedded silts and clays- flood retreat agriculture

fonde very high silt content dry-land cultivation

walo clay-rich soils, sometimes vertisolic- flood-retreat agriculture

SIGNA KAPE colluvial sand over alluvial clay, dry-land farming

SIGNA KHOLE SIGNA BINNE sandy soils- dry-land farming

KATAMAGNE clay soils similar to walo but rarely vertisolic, except where larger depressions retain flood water

NIAWALLE less clay and more sand than katamagne, often formed through sheet wash and colluvium

NIARIKATA minor depressions with more clay

falo river bank

napo small depressions in fonde

fonde levée above maximum flood level

walo depressions behind fonde-flooded annually, sometimes retaining flood water as semi permanent lakes

guillu long sand ridge of dieri

rakhe small basins of interior drainage systems

paraole marginal slopes of rakhe

SENEGAL RIVER

permanence of flooding. Slightly higher in the *walo* areas, and away from the permanent lakes, the soils are submerged from a variable period of 30-120 days and are still rich in clay (30-50%). They are also hydromorphic but not permanently reduced, as in the previous case. Reoxidation is evident during the dry season and this is revealed by mottles in the soil profile. The distinction between *hollalde noir* and *hollalde blanc* in the *walo* areas is reflected in the prevalence and depths of these mottles, the latter being drier and showing mottling at a greater depth. In the *fonde* areas the lower zones of the *fonde noir* contain quantities of clay (20-30%) and increased quantities of silt (15-20%), but are dominantly sandy (50-70%). Periods of inundation of these lower *fonde* areas are variable but generally less than forty days. The higher *fonde* areas, the *fonde blanc* which are never flooded, are again variable in their texture, but are generally more sandy, although in some cases the silt fraction is very important. Where this silt fraction does reach high levels (20% plus), the soil may compact into a very durable crust after the rains and become difficult to work. Despite this, the higher *fonde* areas are more predictable in their hydrology and are therefore used more intensively than the *fonde noir*, which may or may not be flooded, depending on early season rains to the south. Finally, we may distinguish the marginal areas of the Senegal valley and in some cases the deposits of the minor tributaries which lead into it. These contain a mixture of alluvium and colluvium material and are extremely variable in their properties. The Toucouleur term for these areas is the *djedjogol*.

The chemical properties of these different soils are in part a reflection of their texture but also of their position in relation to the hydrology of the valley.

High *fonde* soils are generally alkaline in reaction, retain a mediocre cation exchange capacity and are very variable in their complement of phosphorus. Fluctuations in organic matter are largely due to the condition of the vegetation, which may or may not be cleared, depending upon the local agricultural rotation.

Lower *fonde* soils show increased mottling and have a lower pH, although cation exchange capacity may be slightly higher than those on the high *fonde*. Other characteristics would seem to be similar to the higher *fonde* soils described above. The *hollalde blanc*, or the high *walo* areas, show a great increase in hydromorphic development and an increase in clay content. They are regularly flooded and thus have lower pH values. Their soils are generally more fertile than the low *fonde*, although the figures suggest similar cation exchange capacity and if anything slightly lower phosphorus. This may be due to the fact that these samples were taken from land which is already cultivated and which may therefore be suffering from slight nutrient deficiency. In this context it is interesting to note that those samples taken from well-wooded areas which had not been cultivated tend to suggest greater nutrient enrichment, greater organic matter content and greater levels of phosphorus. The lower *walo* areas are flooded annually and have higher clay percentages and even greater hydromorphic characteristics. Distinctive features are low pH, high cation exchange capacity increasing progressively towards the lowest areas, and generally high phosphorus levels and organic matter content. Again, a difference is noted between those which are cultivated and those which rest under vegetation or fallow, the latter being richer. Finally, the lowest parts of the *walo* bordering the permanent lakes or *khare* show even greater clay development, lower pH and a general continuation in the trends of cation exchange capacity, phosphorus and organic matter, as demonstrated in the previous categories. The colluvial areas bordering the valley have a higher pH and are rich in their nutrient content, although this may be because the samples which were collected in these areas were uncultivated. Table V offers mean values for these principal topographic units which demonstrate the effects just described, whilst complete, individual details can be seen in Appendix F(i).

Table V
Mean values for selected soil properties of Senegal valley soils

Soils derived from:-	pH	CEC	P	C	% sand	% silt	% clay
high **fonde**	6.3	7.9	72.0	1.1	77	12	11
low **fonde**	5.6	14.2	18.2	1.2	52	19	29
high **walo**	5.1	14.9	9.4	1.1	44	30	26
low **walo**	4.7	24.1	38.3	3.2	48	18	34
marginal colluvium	6.5	26.3	11.6	1.7	40	20	40

pH   . $1\text{-}5H_2O$

CEC   :   meq/100 gm a.d.s.

P   : available p.p.m $(NH_4F + HC1)$

C   :   organic C o.d.s.

These alluvial soils are generally fertile, particularly in contrast to other areas of semi-arid Africa, where lack of soil fertility may be a key restraint on crop yields. Table VI gives some general figures for other soils of Africa which contrast strongly with those from the Guidimaka.

Table VI
Selected properties of semi-arid African soils

location	rainfall	pH	CEC	C	% sand	% silt	% clay
Madagascar[a]	c.500	7.8	3.3	0.6	87	3	10
Angola[a]	c.600	6.4	6.3	0.4	85	5	10
Nigeria[a]	c.700	6.7	13.6	0.2	96	0	4
Nigeria[b]	813	6.3	4.3	0.7	—	—	0
Tanzania[c]	874	6.5	8.3	1.4	—	—	20
Tanzania[c]	874	4.9	3.8	0.5	—	—	26
Nigeria[b]	945	7.0	5.6	0.5	—	—	6
Ghana[b]	1043	5.4	8.2	0.7	—	—	19
Senegal[a]	1350	6.5	4.8	1.1	86	5	9
Dahomey[a]	1350	7.2	3.6	1.5	81	6	13

a. D'Hoore (1964)
b. Ahn (1970)
c. Anderson (1957)

The comparison with soils from other parts of semi-arid Africa demonstrates the greater potential of the Guidimakan alluvium as an agricultural resource. Unfortunately, the same cannot be said of the *dieri* soils. With the exception of those derived from the alluvium of the Senegal tributaries, *dieri* soils are characterised by low clay content, low cation exchange capacity and phosphorus content, and poor organic matter retention. Although classified into sand-dune soils, lateritic soils, intermontane soils, etc., an all-embracing mediocrity is noticeable. Table VII illustrates the general poverty of these soils. Full details of individual soil samples from the *dieri* are shown in Appendix F(ii).

In summary, therefore, the soils of the Guidimaka are variable, not only in their mode of origin but also in their agricultural properties. Whilst fertile soils undoubtedly exist, their disjunct distribution, particularly in the interior regions, poses problems of utilisation. The alluvium of the Senegal valley is more continuous, but agricultural development must recognise the peculiar hydrology of the valley and its implication for planning.

Table VII
Mean values for selected soil properties of *dieri* soils

Soils derived from:-	pH	CEC	P	C	% sand	% silt	% clay
sand-dunes	6.6	2.7	28.3	1.0	94	3	3
pediplains	6.3	11.4	22.8	1.2	72	13	15
laterite	5.8	3.1	11.1	0.9	81	10	9
rock outcrops	6.2	7.1	19.2	2.4	79	10	11
alluvium	5.7	23.9	35.5	1.6	45	23	32

II VEGETATION

The following account of the vegetation of the Guidimaka is based upon four weeks' field survey in April 1975, with supplementary observations in July 1976. The timing of this visit was unfortunate, in that it occurred during the latter half of an eight-month dry season. As a consequence of this late date, two major difficulties were encountered:

(a) herb and grass cover had largely disappeared either by grazing or by natural processes of decomposition;

(b) as a result, attention was focused on the tree and shrub vegetation. However, here too loss of leaves and reproductive organs, particularly on the drier areas of the interior, made identification difficult.

The area visited is shown in Figure 5. From this Figure it is obvious that observations were taken not only in the riverine areas of the Guidimaka, but also from its interior as far north as Ndieo on the western margins of the Assaba massif. Similarly, a wide range of observations and samples was taken on the Senegalese bank; again stretching into the interior on to the lateritic plateau of the tertiary sediments. From these observations a broad picture of the major vegetation types emerged, and at a later date, in July 1976, details in the immediate environs of Gouraye, Diaguili and Moulessimou enabled a more sophisticated classification of the vegetation, especially in terms of the soil units described above.

The zonal vegetation of the Sahel and the Sudan and the transition sector is fully described by Trochain (1940), and others at later dates. The importance of the present survey is in its concentration on the azonal vegetation: the influence of the

Senegal river, of the differing soils, and of the varied relief and geology, on an otherwise well-documented vegetation type. The whole of this transition zone is included within the confines of the Guidimaka. In the north, in the region of Ndieo, Dafort and Bouanze, an open thorn bush is prevalent, dominated by *Acacia raddiana* and *Commiphora africana*. Within this formation, localised differences due to soil, topography, and human interference are observed. In the region of villages, *Balanites aegyptiaca* and *Zizyphus mauritiana* become more common. On rocky inselbergs such species as *Pterocarpus lucens* and *Adansonia digitata* can also be found, whilst in the depressions inundated by seasonal rainfall, *Acacia nilotica* and *Mitragyna inermis* tend to dominate. Further to the south, with slightly increased rainfall, *Guiera senegalensis* and *Acacia senegal* begin to replace *Acacia raddiana* and *Commiphora africana*, whilst in the extreme south Sudan savanna, a more dense vegetation with taller trees, is widespread. This savanna type is dominated by *Combretum glutinosum*, with *Pterocarpus lucens* occurring on thin soils and rocky outcrops, and *Grewia bicolor* in depressions. True indicators of more humid conditions experienced in the south can be found as isolated specimens within this general association. Thus *Terminalia spp.*, *Isoberlinia doka*, *Tamarindus indica*, *Boscia angustifolia*, *Khaya senegalensis* and *Acacia sieberiana* are occasionally found.

However, within this broad zonal gradient it is the azonal forms and their relationship to specific conditions of soil and topography which are of greatest importance in this report. In fact, such is the influence of these elements that the general zonal pattern is often completely obscured. A broad dichotomisation is observable between the dry *dieri* and the humid alluvium bordering the rivers. Standing between these two extremes are minor alluvial sediments and colluvium of the interior drainage systems, and those areas within isolated and elevated areas within the Senegal river alluvium which stand above the effects of the local hydrological conditions. Elements of both the dry *dieri* and the Senegal river alluvium can be found in these two units, and in addition there exists a range of plant species which seems to be unique to these types of habitat.

Principal Environments

a. *The* dieri
On many of the elevated plateaux within the region, particularly those of the tertiary sediments of Senegal (south-west of Bakel), but also isolated areas within the Guidimaka, lateritic formations are prominent. These may be in the form of cuirasses, with or

without a veneer of residual material or sand, or they may involve resorted and reconstituted lateritic gravels. On these surfaces the dominant species tends to be *Combretum glutinosum*, with associated *Combretum aculeatum, Sterculia setigera, Lannea humilis, Bombax costatum*, and occasionally *Pterocarpus lucens*. Such associations were found at sites 23, 24 and 31 in Senegal and 54 in the Guidimaka. (See Figure 5 and Appendix F(ii).) Soils are naturally poor, with low cation exchange capacity (2.5),[2] low potassium (0.3 or less) and low magnesium (1.0 or less).

Rocky hills and outcrops produce conditions which are generally similar to that of the laterite, at least in terms of the availability of nutrients and moisture to plants. However, soils derived from richer basaltic sediments can accumulate in small pockets within the rocks and give rise to slightly richer vegetation. Thus, at site 29 soil derived from basaltic material has a high cation exchange capacity (20.6), potassium (0.5) and magnesium (11.8). By contrast, soils developed from the more acid, granitic rocks are poorer, e.g. site 40, with a cation exchange capacity (8.4), potassium (0.4) and magnesium (3.8). On the poorer soils the vegetation is again dominated by *Combretum glutinosum*, though *Pterocarpus lucens* seems to be more abundant than on the laterite, sometimes forming monotypical stands. Other elements, such as *Balanites aegyptiaca* (particularly where human influence is manifest), *Guiera senegalensis, Commiphora africana* (in the north) and occasionally *Adansonia digitata* and *Bombax costatum*, may also be found. Isolated stands of *Sclerocarya birrea* may occur on the marginal slopes of these outcrops, particularly where associated with minor drainage features. The same may be said for *Grewia bicolor*, which also occurs in such situations.

A third terrain form found particularly south and east of the Assaba massif, and often associated with major hills within the Guidimaka generally, are fossil sand-dunes dating from the early quaternary period. These sand-dunes are almost exclusively dominated by *Combretum glutinosum*, although odd specimens of *Terminalia* species may be present. Sites 38 and 39 are typical of this formation. Soil chemistry is again characterised by a low cation exchange capacity (2:3), low potassium (0.2), and low magnesium (1.0 or less). Organic matter retention is also poor.

Whilst these three types form characteristic associations, their areal extent is limited. The majority of the *dieri* consists of undulating intermontane basins and pediplains, and minor fluvial systems. Soil conditions on these surfaces tend to be sandy and may be coincident with the *signa khole* and *signa bine* recognised by local farmers, or may be slightly more clay-rich, relating to the *niarwalle* and *niarikata*, again locally recognised soil types. On the very sandy areas *Combretum glutinosum* may be dominant, but where a small proportion of finer sediments occurs, this species is replaced by *Acacia senegal*, sometimes in association with *Commiphora africana, Lannea humilis* and *Balanites aegyptiaca*. On the *niarikata, Acacia seyal* may increase in proportion to *Acacia senegal*, along with *Guiera senegalensis, Zizyphus mauritiana* and also *Balanites aegyptiaca*. Although not everywhere identifiable, there seems to be a distinction between sandy soils, termed *signa*, which tend to support a greater proportion of *Combretum glutinosum*, and sandy soils which may be included in the general term *niarwalle*, and which tend to be more dominated by *Acacia senegal*.

b. *alluvium*
As itemised above, from the viewpoint of soils and topography, the alluvial lands can be separated into a series of quasi-discrete units with associated soils and vegetation. Thus, the river slopes themselves are normally devoid of vegetation because of the seasonal rise and fall of the river. At the top of this flood limit, lines of *Parkinsonia aculeata* are often found, although this species is not native to Africa. On the *fonde* a range of species exists and forms complex and subtle associations. Nearest the river, isolated specimens of *Ficus* and *Lonchocarpus* species, *Celtis integrifolia*, and other standard trees can be found. These are dominant along the front of the *fonde* but may occur as isolated specimens within a complex association of *Zizyphus mucronata, Zizyphus mauritiana* and *Bauhinia rufescens* on the *fonde* top, *Guiera senegalensis* on the back slope, merging into *Maytenus senegalensis* and *Piliostigma reticulatum* on the lower levels. As the soils become more clay-rich and merge into the *walo* areas, the *Guiera senegalensis* stands become thinner and are replaced by *Mitragyna inermis* and ultimately *Acacia nilotica* and *Mimosa asperata*, the last surrounding the permanent lakes or *khare*. The dominance of individual species within these mixed associations is very much controlled by soil texture and available moisture.

c. *Transitional areas*
Between the alluvium of the Senegal valley and the *dieri* of the interior there exists a mixture of terrain forms which owe their character not only to these two major units, but also to the inclusion of individual forms unique to these particular associations. For the most part the merging of the rear slopes of the *walo* with the drier *signa* to the interior, or with the *rakhe/paraole* of

interior drainage systems, gives rise to terrain which supports a vegetation type including both alluvial and *dieri* elements. However, where the marigots of these drainage systems are large and abut against ridges or inselbergs, additional elements are included. This may be due in part to the fact of their particular juxtaposition, i.e. that between the marigot and the rocky hills, but may also be a result of the fact that these areas tend to be furthest from the riverside villages and are therefore little cultivated. As a result, dense riverine, gallery woodlands occasionally with 20-25 m. specimens of *Acacia sieberiana, Diospyros mespiliformis, Khaya senegalensis* and *Terminalia macroptera* are found. A lower storey of *Acacia nilotica, Combretum micranthum, Grewia bicolor* and other straggling shrubs may be present. The whole woodland is often very dense and frequently overhangs the marigot to give a deep shade that is unique in the area and represents an additional vegetation-landform association. Sites 25-28 and 22 are fairly characteristic of this type of vegetation. Because of the increased humidity associated with these marigots, Sudanic elements are often present. Thus *Khaya senegalensis, Diospyros mespiliformis* and *Anogeissus leiocarpus* are perhaps more typical of the more humid Sudan savannas to the south than those of the more arid Sahel.

The sometimes imperceptible changes that take place in the vegetation as topographic and soil condition alter are best examined through a series of transects, which highlight the complexities of these associations and their close relationship to specific soil and soil-water properties.

2. Vegetation Gradients

Three transects are offered here to give an indication of the pattern of vegetation communities which exist both in the alluvial areas and on the marginal zones between the alluvium and *dieri*. These gradients are represented in schematic form, Figure 7, showing three vegetation-topographic profiles with additional soil information.

As a result of information gained from these transect studies, and from a general appraisal of the vegetation of the region, specific preferences for each plant species can be itemised. These are given in Table VIII.

Fig. 7 Simplified transects of the Guidimakan riverine area
demonstrating the relationship between vegetation and soils

1 *Acacia nilotica*

2 *Acacia seyal*

3 *Acacia sieberiana*

4 *Bauhinia rufescens*

5 *Capparis decidua*

6 *Combretum glutinosum*

7 *Grewia bicolor*

8 *Guiera senegalensis*

9 *Maytenus senegalensis*

10 *Mitragyna inermis*

11 *Piliostigma reticulatum*

12 *Zizyphus mauritiana*

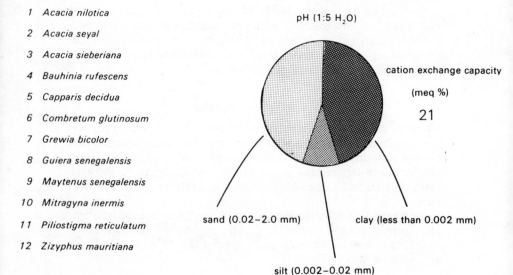

4·9

pH (1:5 H$_2$O)

cation exchange capacity

(meq %)

21

sand (0.02–2.0 mm)

clay (less than 0.002 mm)

silt (0.002–0.02 mm)

Table VIII
Habitats of principal trees of the Guidimaka

species	local name	habitat
Mimosa asperata		margins of permanent lakes in *fonde*
Acacia nilotica	*diebe*	throughout major depressions, inundated for 30-120 days; hydro-morphic clay-rich soils; along oueds in the *dieri* and wherever inundation occurs
Mitragyna inermis	*khile*	often occurs with **Acacia nilotica**, although in drier positions; may also be found as an outer zone (behind **Mimosa asperata**) around *fonde* lakes
Acacia seyal	*saye*	prefers clay-rich soils, though not flooded; thus, found at interior margins of depressions, or similar soil and topographic positions in the *dieri* (*katamagne, rakhe, paraole*) also found in *fonde* associations, possible where soils contain silt
Acacia senegal	*dibe*	occurs on sandier soils than **Acacia seyal**, principally in the *dieri* (*niarwalle*); in minor depressions in the *dieri*, where soils are transitional between *niarwalle* and *katamagne*, occurs in association with **Acacia seyal**
Piliostigma reticulatum	*yafe*	found in two positions: on margins of *katamagne* and *signa* (*signa kape*), and on margins of *fonde* and *walo*; generally an indication of increased soil moisture
Combretum glutinosum	*tefe*	the characteristic zonal species, occurring in a wide range of arid soils; forms monotypical stands on sandy soils (*signa khole, signa bine*), but also on lateritic and skeletal soils
Combretum micranthum		generally restricted to small depressions and channel banks in lateritic, or thin-soiled areas
Guiera senegalensis	*khame*	the typical plant of the *fonde*, preferring soils with median moisture status; often found in association with **Piliostigma reticulatum**, particularly on *fonde-walo* margins
Maytenus senegalensis	*sansambane*	not widespread but indicative of the subtle moisture gradients of the *fonde-walo* and *dieri-walo*; occurs in slightly more moist sites than **Guiera senegalensis**

species	local name	habitat
Capparis decidua	sombitte	normally found in the *dieri*, in colluvial-alluvial soils with intermediate moisture status (lower areas of *niarwalle*, margins of *katamagne*
Grewia bicolor	sambe	a *dieri* species, requiring a moisture status similar to or greater than **Capparis decidua**; usually on skeletal soils or lithosols; often close to channel banks where rock outcrops are seen
Pterocarpus lucens	bambagne	occurring in drier sites than those preferred by **Grewia bicolor**, but again associated with lithosols; may form monotypical stands on rocky hills or ridges
Sterculia setigera		similar preference to **Pterocarpus lucens**, but occurring as isolated specimens and prominent on lateritic soils
Lannea humilis	dinguindongue	nowhere widespread, but associated with **Pterocarpus lucens** and **Sterculia setigera** on skeletal or thin colluvial soils in the *dieri*
Commiphora africana		dry, thin soils of the *dieri*; localised
Acacia macrostachya		associated with poor lateritic soils of the *dieri*, but always close to channels, particularly gully forms
Bombax costatum		lower slopes of inselbergs in the southern part of the Guidimaka
Balanites aegyptiaca	sekhene	most widespread as a post-cultural disturbance species; tolerates a wide range of soils particularly just above the upper limit of flooding on the *fonde*
Zizyphus species	fa fa mbine tarun fa	three species recognised, though habitat preferences not known; generally on drier *fonde* sites and as post-cultural invading species
Bauhinia rufescens	gassambe	generally confined to *fonde* sites in association with **Guiera senegalensis** and **Piliostigma reticulatum**

NOTES

1 In the text and illustrations, the Toucouleur distinction of high and low *walo* lands is used, *hollalde blanc* or *hollalde ranere*, the higher *walo*, whilst the lower component is termed *hollalde noir* or *hollalde wallere*.
2 These and similar figures for cation content in the text are expressed in miliequivalents per hundred grams of air-dry soil (MEQ/100gm. a.d.s.).

CHAPTER 5

Settlement and Communications

Estimates of the total population of the Guidimaka are given in Chapter 2, Part II, and while at best inaccurate, they nevertheless suggest a population density of between five and ten persons per square kilometre. The region is, therefore, sparsely populated by any standards.

The settlement pattern of the Guidimaka would seem at first glance to be more or less evenly dispersed (see Figure 8). However, two factors modify this apparent pattern. Firstly, the location of villages is for the most part determined by the availability of water and, secondly, the differing economics of the villages modifies the type of water supply that is regarded as minimal. An agricultural village requires a considerable supply of water and suitable alluvial farm lands. Thus, the larger Soninke settlements are located close to the alluvial plains of the Senegal river itself, or its major tributaries such as the Garfa, Niorde and Karakoro. Conversely, the much smaller, and often semi-permanent settlements of the nomadic Peul and Maure herdsmen are situated in accordance with dry-season grazing and a less demanding water supply. Locations are more scattered and as often associated with minor fluvial systems and interfluves as with major valleys that are required by settled agriculturalists.

Most villages support fewer than a thousand people, at least in the Département of Selibabi (Kane and Lericollais, 1974), although much larger settlements exist, particularly by virtue of antiquity and the presence of extensive agricultural land. Thus, Diaguili, Woumpou, Diogountourou and Selibabi contain well over two thousand people, whilst further north Hassi-Chaggar, Dafort and Bouanze are of similar size. Such population estimates are less than perfect, and should be viewed as denoting relative differences rather than absolute values. The majority of the largest villages are sustained by an agricultural economy. Those settlements which support herding economies are generally smaller, particularly in the western sector of the Département of Selibabi, where Peul villages of fewer than five hundred people are the norm. These latter are usually located inland from the best agricultural land of the Senegal, Garfa and Niorde alluvium, often along the feeder streams which drain into the larger valleys. In these locations easy access to both the grazing lands of the *dieri* and the water supplies of the smaller tributaries is possible.

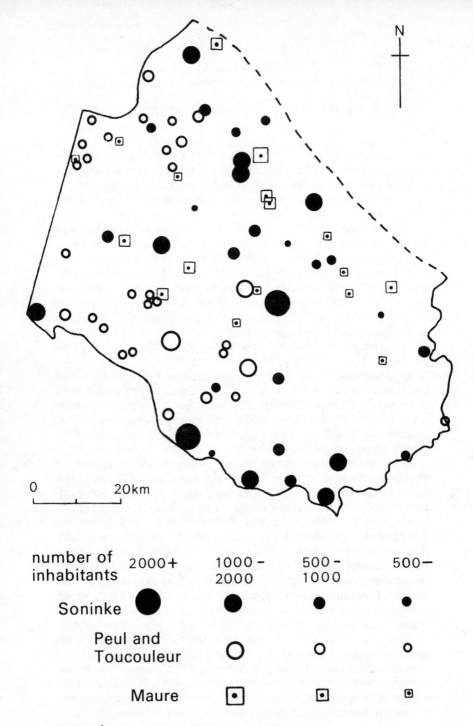

N

0   20km

number of
inhabitants   2000+   1000-   500-   500-
                        2000   1000

Soninke

Peul and
Toucouleur

Maure

Fig. 8 Département of Selibabi: distribution of population

The Guidimaka is dominated by four groups of people: the Soninke and Toucouleur agriculturalists, and the Peul and Maure herdsmen. Figures for the Département of Selibabi (Kane and Lericollais, 1974) suggest a population of 44,000, of whom 24,000 are Soninke, 11,700 are Maure, and 6300 and 2000 Peul and Toucouleur respectively. Within the Département, approximately 70 per cent of the Soninke are located along the Senegal and Niorde valleys. Further north a similar concentration is noted in the Garfa system, with major settlements such as Ajar-Sarakole, Oulombome, Dafort, Bouanze and Ndieo.

The presence of Bambara people working as salaried labourers in numerous villages of the region is a fact of some significance. Kane and Lericollais (1974) do not provide figures of the size of this immigrant population (largely from Mali), but suggest a figure of 1,005 Bambara for the Arrondissement of Ololdou near Bakel in Senegal. Doubtless, the presence of Bambara in the Guidimaka, in numbers as yet unspecified, bears witness to the 'drain' on the work-force resulting from emigration of the Soninke from the area. We shall return to the question of immigrant salaried labour in Part II.

As mentioned above, the stock-rearing Maure and Peul settlements are smaller and more scattered, the latter particularly so. Peul villages are concentrated in the west, whilst Maure settlements are more northern and eastern in their distribution (Figure 8). The classification of each village according to its predominant group obscures a level of heterogeneity which is certainly evident at Gouraye, where both Maure and Soninke people are also found. The largest of the villages of the region is Diaguili, with an estimated population in excess of four thousand. It is thus comparable in size with Selibabi, the regional administrative centre. Whilst Diaguili is exclusively Soninke, the population of Selibabi is more heterogeneous and contains all four ethnic groups. With the possible exception of some of the other, larger centres such as Bouanze and Dafort in the northern department of Ould Yenze, all other villages are considerably smaller. One might view a typical agricultural village with good soil resources and a degree of antiquity as having a population of between one and two thousand.

Whilst the location of villages is to a large degree determined by the potentials of the environment, their size is not unconnected to the communication system of the region. Although it would be unreasonable to ascribe the size to which the larger villages have grown to their location along principal routes (the reverse may well provide a better explanation), the connection between the two is evident. In general, the road or, rather, track network is at best inadequately developed. Not only is the Guidimaka poorly connected with the rest of Mauritania, but communications within the region itself are very precarious.

Roads which enable the movement of motor vehicles throughout the year are few. The Mbout-Selibabi-Kiffa road, and those between Selibabi and Gouraye and Selibabi and Baediam, complete this group. Of the remaining links of the communications network, only the Selibabi to Maghama and Selibabi to Diaguili tracks are open to vehicular traffic during the rainy season (albeit irregularly). Nowhere else in the region is motor access possible during the wet season. Indeed, motor vehicles are a rarity in the Guidimaka; people travel by horse, mule or on foot. Even bicycles are infrequently seen.

The settlement pattern and communication system of the Guidimaka is one of scattered, isolated villages. Access to centres outside the region, or indeed between villages within it, is limited.

PART II
Analysis

A distinctive feature of the present-day Guidimaka is the importance of workers' migration to France. Any analysis of the overall situation or an attempt at a general diagnosis should therefore give due consideration to this phenomenon.

CHAPTER 6

From Isolation to Exile

Our first concern is to recall the historical process which has led to the present situation. In order to do this, it is necessary to consider the Guidimaka within the wider geographic zone of the Upper Senegal valley.

The river was the main axis of French colonial penetration into West Africa. With more than 1000 km. navigable when in spate, for nearly three centuries after the seventeenth century it was 'the key to the early French trading, in gum arabic, slaves, bees-wax, raw hides, etc.' (Seck, 1965, p.72). Until the middle of the nineteenth century, only the lower reaches were involved in this trading. However, the construction of Bakel fort in 1953-54 (as well as several others downstream, such as Matam and Podor) opened the upper river in its turn for trading under the protection of the military. 'Trading through Bakel in 1856 consisted of several hundred tonnes of gum arabic, two tonnes of hides, groundnuts, millet, 192 kilogrammes of ivory and only 78 grammes of Gold' (idem, p.73). However, it was only after the bloody suppression of the Soninke revolt led by Mamadou Lamine Drame in 1886-88 that French domination was established beyond challenge.

Thus, at the end of the nineteenth century, Bakel became for some decades 'the major economic centre of the Upper Senegal, before this role was taken over by Kayes' (idem, p.81). It owed its pre-eminence to 'its position at the crossroads between the Soninke lands of Ngoye and Mauritanian Guidimaka, which produce gum arabic, millet, and groundnuts' (idem).

The main suppliers of gum arabic were the Maures on the Mauritanian bank of the river. It was collected by their slaves and brought by themselves to the trading posts. As for groundnuts and millet, they were produced by Soninke farmers living beside the river, or in the surrounding inland areas on the Senegalese side. The groundnuts which were intended for export were sent to St. Louis (at a rate of five to six thousand tonnes per year). The millet went several ways: part was sent to St. Louis, part was used to feed local garrisons, and the rest was bartered to the Maures in exchange for gum arabic.[1]

Towards the end of the last century, the Upper Senegal region became involved in colonial trading systems. However, the use of money seems to have been rather limited. Transactions frequently took the form of direct exchange between local produce and imported goods (idem, p.82).

This relative prosperity was none the less short-lived. The fall in the price of groundnuts between 1883-84, and then of gum arabic at the beginning of the twentieth century (through competition with that produced in the Sudano-Egyptian Kordofan) led to a rapid decline in the volume of trade.

During the same period, a large part of the goods traffic using the Senegal river gradually shifted to the railway which was under construction between Dakar and Niger (the Thies-Kayes link was completed in 1923). With the extension of the railway, groundnut cultivation spread, with the result that economic activity as a whole gradually moved southwards.

A small trade in gum arabic and millet was all that remained. Even if the valley's reputation as a 'millet granary' has been somewhat overstated, until recently considerable quantities of grain went to feed the inhabitants of the large urban agglomerations. Twenty years ago, the annual traffic was approximately fifteen to twenty thousand tonnes (Boutillier and Canterelle, 1962). This estimate refers more particularly to the middle valley of the river. None the less, it is certain that the upper valley was also affected, at least partially, by these commercial trends. However, this was not enough to sustain much economic activity. One by one, the trading posts of the large companies of St. Louis, Kayes and Dakar were closed down. The final blow was delivered by the crisis throughout West Africa during the Second World War. The upper valley of the river (on both banks) gradually closed in on itself, isolated from those important economic and technical changes which affected regions to the south.

The geographical zone in which we are interested is the Mauritanian Guidimaka, yet most of our remarks so far concern Bakel, which is on the Senegalese bank. This results from the fact that when the French conquered the upper valley only the land nearest the river was occupied by sedentary farmers. During the nineteenth century, the insecurity engendered by successive wars, and particularly by attacks from the Maures,[2] had led the Soninke to seek the shelter of the river. At the end of the century, only 'some villages in the interior remained: Guemou, which was fortified by the Toucouleurs of El Hadj Omar and then destroyed by the colonial troups, Koumba Ndao and above all, Selibabi, 30 km. from the river, which had 5000 inhabitants in 1890: an important trading centre where the Maures exchanged their cattle for Soninke cereals' (Kane and Lericollais, 1974, p.15). It was only after 1890, after the crushing of the revolt led by Mamadou Lamine Drame, that settlement on the right bank spread well into the interior. This movement was a response to a need for population 'decongestion' through the opening up of new land; but it also represented the desire to flee beyond the reach of the violence and exactions of the colonial power. The movement of the Soninke was almost complete by 1923, and the list of villages of this ethnic group given in a monograph on the Guidimaka dating from that period (Saint Pere, 1925) corresponds to the list one would draw up today (with a few exceptions, most notably Tachota Barane and Tachota Botokholo). The movement into the area by the Peul (Fulani), Toucouleur and Maure took place over a much longer period. Movements of population and the creation of new, temporary encampments are still occurring today, particularly following the recent years of drought.

Thus, the interior of the country was not brought into cultivation until after the brief period of prosperity of 'the riverine areas'.[3] The agriculture which developed there did so in the absence of the pressures which in other parts of Africa led to a constant increase in the cultivation of so-called 'cash crops' intended for market exchange.

In their landholdings, farmers gave priority to food crops (sorghum and millet, maize and rice), leaving cotton and groundnuts only a marginal place, which corresponded strictly to their own consumption needs. In 1920, Saint-Pere (idem) estimated that the area devoted to cereals in the 'Cercle' of the Guidimaka comprised as much as 16,400 hectares, whilst the areas under groundnuts and cotton were not much more than a thousand hectares. Although the accuracy of these estimates may well be questioned, there is no doubt that they are valid as an indication of the priorities assigned to different crops.

Certainly there were commercial exchanges involving agricultural produce, but they took place almost totally within the framework of the traditional markets dominated by the Maures, and took the form of barter exchange (salt for millet, millet for gum arabic) rather than through monetary transactions.

To summarise, it was an economy where only small amounts of cash circulated, but where, none the less, the colonial system was exerting its usual pressure on the local inhabitants to possess cash, particularly through taxation. It was certainly not through the small quantity of agricultural produce which the trading companies were prepared to buy that this needed cash could be raised. This need for money, even if limited, and the difficulties in obtaining it locally, provided the necessary conditions to stimulate a migratory movement towards more promising regions and activities. The Soninke have a long history of travel, particularly as a result of their long-distance trade with the south. More recently, work as hands on river boats, then on seagoing ships, gave the inhabitants of the riverine villages of the Senegal valley (particularly Diaguili) the chance to go further afield in search of remunerative work. But it was particularly with the growth of groundnuts production in the central Senegalese basin that a strong and sustained pull began to be exerted on the whole of the active population of this neglected area.

Under the strong influence of the large trading houses, effectively backed by the colonial administration, groundnut cultivation entered a period of vigorous and rapid growth. As the railway advanced, new land was opened up for cultivation, causing a strong demand for labour from surrounding regions. So began the seasonal migration of those workers known as *navetanes*. Large numbers of them were Soninke, particularly from the Guidimaka.

In most cases, these farmers did not work as hired labourers in the usual sense of the term. They normally rented a plot from a landowner who also supplied them with groundnut seed and the necessary tools for clearing and cultivation. In return, the *navetanes* had to work four days a week for their 'boss'. They also had to reimburse the seed at an interest rate varying from 50 per cent to 100 per cent.

This movement of labour was doubly profitable for the commercial interests at work in Senegal. On the one hand, it was much less costly to let the workers come on their own initiative (and at their own expense!) to work the land near the main axes of communication, than to encourage them to farm in their home areas. In the latter case they would then be obliged to collect the produce locally, in difficult conditions (tracks being in a deplorable state) and at great expense. On the other hand, it is certain that the cash revenues obtained by the *navetanes* largely contributed to sustaining the sales activities of the trading posts in their home areas, particularly in the trading towns along the river.

Having nothing else to sell to the trading houses, the farmers of Upper Senegal and the Guidimaka[4] were progressively brought to 'exporting' their own kin.

However, as the years went by, the growth of a resident population in the groundnut basin of Senegal, aided perhaps by the slow but effective spread of animal traction equipment, lessened the seasonal demand for labour from the river area. The flow of migration, far from drying up, however, gradually took another direction. The pull on rural labour exercised by cities with their relative diversification of activities reorientated these migratory movements towards the large agglomerations, and especially towards the more important centres of Dakar and Abidjan. However, employment possibilities did not grow as fast as the influx of workers, and unemployment grew. From the 'fifties, the slums, full of uprooted people living from day to day, spread more widely. It was clear from then on that the image of city employment and prosperity was far removed from the reality, and that all those who were deluded would see their difficulties increase rather than diminish.

It was at this time in the 'sixties that new routes of migration were opened, taking workers to more distant destinations outside Africa: to Europe and, above all, to France.

This was no chance happening. This evolution was the consequence of the strong demand for foreign labour which accompanied France's period of economic growth and industrialisation at the end of the 'fifties. In spite of its distance, and although to a far lesser degree than some Mediterranean and North African countries, French-speaking West Africa responded to this demand.

A more specific question arises, however. Why were the Soninke so much more susceptible than other ethnic groups to this attraction? Why, out of the sixty to seventy thousand African workers recently counted in France, were 65 per cent Soninke (from Mali, Mauritania and Senegal), and only 15 per cent Toucouleur (Dubresson, 1974)? On this precise point it seems indisputable that the role of certain individuals who came from some large Soninke villages along the river has been decisive. Amongst the very first group of migrants, who had been sailors for many years (both on the big commercial ships, and on the smaller boats of petty traders of all shades) close links were maintained with important members of the Marseilles milieu. The latter, already familiar with many other forms of illicit trade, rapidly grasped the advantage they could gain from the situation, and used them as hustlers and recruiting agents all along the African coast. By this they were able to procure the cheap labour which had suddenly become such a sought-after commodity for French industry.[5] 'Thus becomes apparent the channel which leads [the migrant] from Dakar or Abidjan to Marseilles: he has necessarily to go through the representative of some "barbot" from Marseilles' (Dia Moukari, 1965). As a former migrant declared: 'An important Soninke trader obtains the aeroplane tickets for those who have no papers. He acts as travel agent and demands a sum of 140,000 to 150,000 cfa[6], (IDEP, 1972, p.50). Given the key role they played in the network thus established, it followed naturally that the Soninke intermediaries should direct their recruitment firstly among their own kin. Was it not a privilege for a jobless man, after vegetating for months in Dakar, to find work incomparably better-paid, even if thousands of miles away, than he could hope to find if he remained where he was in spite of the exploitation of which he would become victim and of which he was usually unaware?

The 'specialisation' of the Soninke, which occurred in the beginning in a slightly fortuitous manner (although it was no accident that some of them were led to seek work as sailors from the beginning of the century) then generated its own self-sustaining momentum. As the formalities for entering France became more and more difficult, the fact of having on the spot a relative, a friend, or a mutual-aid society which could obtain a work contract from an employer in France, constituted an increasing advantage. [7] However strongly other ethnic groups may wish to migrate today, it is certain that they will come up against a type of de facto monopoly, into which penetration is extremely difficult.

NOTES

1 Trading of gum arabic was an ancient tradition of the Maures; they also used it to feed their slaves who gathered it.
2 These raids were, to a large extent, a result of the slave trade and conflicts brought on by the colonial advance.
3 Such prosperity was relative and would not have benefited all sections of society. No doubt the Maure slaves received little reward for their efforts in harvesting gum arabic.
4 We are focusing here on the Guidimaka and the Upper Senegal, but it is obvious that the phenomena evoked here affected much larger areas of Africa — notably the whole valley of the Senegal as well as regions of Mali.
5 The organisation of immigration networks to France proved to be a profitable venture for certain unscrupulous people, and not only in the case of Africans: many Portuguese workers have had this unhappy experience.
6 Roughly £285 to £330, with 450 cfa to the £ sterling.
7 It is estimated that 80 per cent of Malians and 75 per cent of Senegalese now in France found their jobs through 'friends' (IDEP, 1972, p.79).

CHAPTER 7

Present Problems of Migration

I ITS MAGNITUDE AND ITS SPATIAL PATTERN

We have two fairly detailed studies on migration from the various villages of the Département of Selibabi (Kane and Lericollais, 1974; Dussauze-Ingrand, n.d.). It is on the basis of these, supplemented in places by our own personal observations, that we present a review of the problem.

The first difficulty lies in estimating the total population of the Département. Available information is contradictory, as we have already seen. We have the following estimates:

35,577 inhabitants, according to the 'Tableau de Commande-ment' (administrative statistics) of the Préfecture of Selibabi.

44,208 inhabitants, according to the study of Kane and Lericollais (op. cit.).

48,000 inhabitants, according to the study of Dussauze-Ingrand (n.d.).

A list that we were able to consult at the Statistics Office in Nouakchott — only extracts of which were available to us — sugesting finally a population of well over 50,000.

There is obviously some room for improvement in the accuracy of these figures!

When it comes to evaluating the number of migrants from the area, the problem is identical: Dussauze-Ingrand (op.cit.) estimates a total of 3,000 for the Département (on the basis of the distribution of money-orders and family allowances); Lericollais (op.cit.), for his part, following a village-by-village field study, counted 2,513.

Depending on the total population estimate used, the ratio of migrants to the total population varies from more than 8 per cent to less than 5 per cent — a difference of nearly 100 per cent!

In fact, this overall estimate does not mean very much in itself. We give it here only to stress that figures should be handled with great care. In conditions of such uncertainty, simple qualitative approximations provide a better basis for understanding than calculations of an apparent, but false, numerical precision.

If we adhere to the estimates given in Kane and Lericollais' study (the most reliable, since they are based on fieldwork), at least we can arrive at meaningful estimates of the extent of migration. Most noteworthy was the finding that one third of the active male population of the Soninke villages studied was absent in 1973 — a large majority being in France. This indicates a severe drain on the work-force of the village communities.

Over and above this confirmation of a state of affairs that has frequently been observed, two particular findings of this study seem important to note.

First is the fact already suggested by the historical analysis, that it was from the 'sixties onwards that the migratory movement had its biggest growth. At the same time, the majority of migrants tended to come from the younger male age group, 15-25 years old. It seems in these conditions that: 'The drain operates more and more clearly in those age-groups approaching working age: departures at 16, 17, 18 years are becoming customary' (Kane and Lericollais, op.cit., p.7). It is well and truly the vital forces of the villages which are being sapped.

Secondly, the geographical distribution of migration levels reveals, in the Département of Selibabi, the existence of two distinct zones: 'For the approximately 35,000 inhabitants of the riverine villages,[1] the mean emigration ratio is 35 per cent, and in no village is it lower than 25 per cent; whereas in the twenty Soninke villages of the northern zone, the average ratio of emigration is 16 per cent; between individual villages, the ratios are extremely variable, going from less than 10 per cent to more than 50 per cent' (idem, p.4). The antiquity of the migratory phenomenon equally clearly distinguishes the riverine villages from those in the north: 'Some migrants from the villages along the river left over twenty years ago, and then the departures increased in the early 'sixties. Migration has kept up a high level until now, whereas the villages in the north have been supplying migrants for only ten years.' (idem, p.7). Figure 9 illustrates the intensity of emigration for the majority of settlements in the Département de Selibabi and the Arrondissement d'Ololdou in Senegal, and clearly shows the influence of the river and communication links. We shall see later how far this difference between riverine zones and zones in the interior of the Guidimaka is reflected in numerous other areas (physical environment and land-use patterns, most notably). Thus, in the precise case of emigration, everything seems to have happened as if an available 'reserve' labour force had been gradually exploited as the intensity of demand increased. One should state, however, that the distinction between the two zones, as with all clear-cut divisions, is in some respects arbitrary. In a more refined analysis, one would have to take into account such nuances as the proximity of a road (as is the case with Agouemit

53

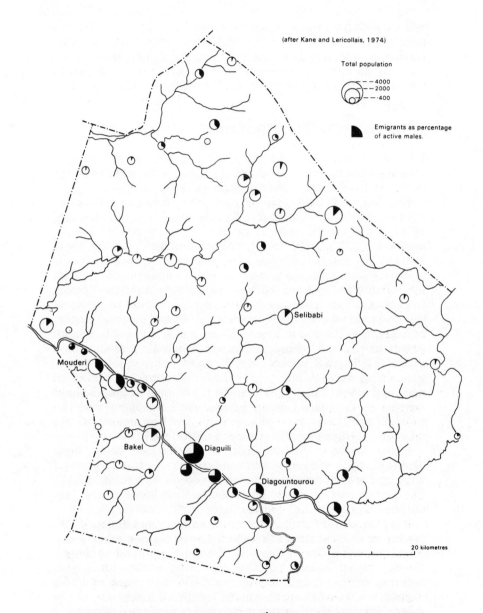

Fig. 9 Emigration and population of the Département of Selibabi (Mauritania) and the Arrondissement d'Ololdou (Senegal) in 1972

54

and Oulombome, situated more than 60 km. from the river, yet none the less having important migration ratios). On the other hand, the difference is accentuated as soon as one moves away from the main axes of communication. This applies particularly to the Soninke villages situated at the foot of the Assaba massif.

II MONETARY FLOWS LINKED TO MIGRATION

The second major characteristic of the migratory phenomenon, a counterpart to the drain on human resources, is the important flow of money from France into the migrants' areas of origin.

The migrants hold very menial jobs: labourers, unskilled workers, particularly concentrated in the car industry (Dubresson, 1974). Their average wage is extremely low (about 910 FF per month in 1972 (IDEP, 1972)), though doubtless slightly above 1,000 FF per month nowadays. This calculation of wages actually received should take into account periods of unemployment, since job stability for migrant workers, particularly for those coming from black Africa, has always been extremely low. Non-employment (the true ratio between migrants without jobs and the total number of migrants in France) is around 20 per cent (idem, p.93). Several studies carried out before the current economic recession have shown that migrant workers very frequently change jobs; once a year on average (idem, p.73) with, each time, a period of non-employment longer than a month.[2] Without doubt, the large increase in unemployment in France will have aggravated this situation over the last two years. One can therefore assume that the migrant's average monthly income is still below 1,000 FF.

Living in very difficult material conditions, many times described, these workers achieve the remarkable feat of saving a large part of their earnings; as much as 40 per cent (idem, p.143). The greater part of this is sent back to their home villages, for purposes which we shall consider later on.

It is obviously difficult to determine an accurate estimate of the magnitude of these money flows to the home areas, especially as it is sent through different channels. The most important of these is through postal orders, but they also send money home with returning migrants, and may take some in cash when returning themselves. Transfers are also made, by special agreement, by the French government department responsible for family allowances to their equivalents in the migrants' countries of origin. The authors of the IDEP study estimated that monetary transfers linked to migration for the whole of Mauritania in a recent year[3] reached a total of 1 billion 450 million cfa or 290 million Ouguiyas.[4] This same study showed that this figure is higher than the average annual aid in loans and grants received by Mauritania between 1963 and 1968. These estimates are of course open to improvement, but they do allow us to appreciate the size of the monetary contribution which migration represents for the national economy. Once again we are reminded that emigration is no chance happening, to be explained at the level of the responses and mentality of individuals. It is a social and economic reality of great consequence, with an impact at the level of the national economy.

If we confine our attention to the home region, we also have some estimates of the importance of the monetary flow into the Département of Selibabi. Dussauze-Ingrand (op.cit.), in her study, proposes a first estimate of 335 million cfa (67 million Ouguiyas) for 1970-71.[5] She based her calculations on the official figures of monetary transfers, postal and others. If we concern ourselves with the statements of migrants and their families regarding the quantity of the annual remittances per worker, we arrive at a much higher figure. In fact, the facts that we have gathered in the field, which confirm the findings of Dussauze-Ingrand, suggest 40,000[6] Ouguiyas as the average minimum annual remittance per migrant.[7] In the riverine villages, and in particular Diaguili, where emigration is much longer-established and where 'seamen' earning relatively high wages are fairly numerous, the level of remittances is much higher and can be more than 80,000 Ouguiyas per migrant.

On the basis of 200,000 cfa per migrant working in France for more than two years (the first two years being devoted to paying off the debts incurred for the first trip), Dussauze-Ingrand (op.cit.) obtains a second global estimate of 480,000[8] million cfa (96 million Ouguiyas) for the Département of Selibabi. Even if her estimate of 3,000 migrants from this Département seems rather high, particularly compared to the figures provided by Kane and Lericollais (op.cit.), we can still assume that the amount for the whole of the 10th Region of Mauritania (which includes the two Départments of Selibabi and Ould Yenze) is considerably higher. In any case, it seems that the figure of 100 million Ouguiyas[9] would be a reasonable estimate of the annual remittances by the migrants from the 10th Region.

We must not forget that such calculations can be wildly inaccurate.[10] Too much importance should not be given to the figures in this context because of their apparent numerical precision. At the most, they constitute the elements of a qualitative appreciation. In any case, for the level of analysis that we need

56

here, there is no necessity for an exact estimate. Even if the figure of 100 million Ouguiyas were to be halved, the fact would still remain that emigration provides a monetary contribution incomparably larger than any other, whether it be state payments or subsidies, or even more so the revenues from an agriculture within which a market sector is very small.

As we shall see, even if the effects of this massive injection of money are far from positive, one can hardly condemn migration merely for the sake of theoretical or moral principles. Emigration is a fact. Financially it offers those who participate immeasurably greater advantages than any other substitute activity that could at the moment be proposed for their areas of origin. Moreover, as has been many times underlined, even if the scandalous conditions in which African workers in France live make their stay both physically and psychologically difficult,[11] the migrants whom we have met in the villages have generally shown an ambivalent attitude to their overseas experience. The memory of the hardships they had suffered are often counterbalanced in their minds (at least, with the younger ones) by the prestige of 'modern' living. Although, for exiles living in a sordid immigrants' hostel ('foyer'), homesickness for the country of their birth is very strong, those whom we met in their villages did not appear to be particularly daunted by the prospect of setting out again. However unpleasant the migrant's experience may be: separation from his family, the need to live in a foreign and often hostile social environment, extremely tough living and working conditions; however strong may be his desire to remain with his kin at home, in most cases he is far from being ready to accept just any alternative solution.

III THE DISTRIBUTION AND USE OF THE MONEY

Whilst any estimates of the overall amount of money injected into the local economy by migration are uncertain and very approximate, our knowledge is little better when it comes to the actual use to which these sums are put.

Like others before us, we were able to gather a certain amount of qualitative information during our stay in the Guidimaka. However, experience elsewhere has shown us that where economic behaviour is concerned, there is often a considerable gap between actual practice and public statements (the latter often reflecting socially accepted conventions). In fact, it is only by studying budgets in the minutest detail that we could arrive at a precise knowledge of the way the money saved by migrants is actually spent.

Nevertheless, bearing in mind that what we are attempting is to establish the main threads of an overall diagnosis, it is once again possible to approach the problem from the basis of reasonable approximation. By this we are able to emphasise certain principal factors which, from our existing knowledge, will enable us to determine the central orientation of a development programme.

Within this perspective, the problem of the use of income falls into two separate parts: the first concerns the effective control of the money, and the second the main uses to which the money is put.

The question of knowing who exercises control over the money from migration is certainly the more complex of the two, and is not easily answered. In fact, although a worker living in France draws his wage himself, and is therefore theoretically free to use it as he wishes, it is clear that in reality he is subject to collective pressures which are difficult to withstand.

Many young men go to France on the initiative of their families; parents or elder brothers. In such cases, they are duty-bound to return to them a large part of their wages. As we have seen in recent years, young men between seventeen and eighteen years of age have increased as a proportion of the total number of migrants. Very often, their initial departure is financed by an older man, who also helps to find work. In many cases they are directly under his 'tutelage', and hand over to him all their wages, save a small amount of pocket money for themselves. As has often been stressed (Diarra, 1964; Dubresson, op.cit., in particular), the milieu of African workers living in France presents a very strong degree of social cohesion, and this is particularly true of the Soninke. Traditional hierarchies and norms of behaviour (in questions of social status, family relationships, religious practices) remain very much alive within groups, which often tend to reflect their home communities.[12] In such a setting, social control is obviously very strong. Living in daily contact with their elders, it is difficult for the young to escape family authority. Even an older man, in theory more free, finds himself constrained by group pressure to continue to play the role of a 'good son' or 'good husband' and to remain faithful to his 'family duties'. Often, the remittance of money is collectively organised, through a common fund or 'tontine', which greatly reduces the scope for personal initiative. The only way to escape these pressures is to leave the common hostel and lead an independent life. Some (an increasing number it seems) do attempt this, but by so doing they also deprive themselves of the material and emotional security of group living. There is a choice to be made and it is far from simple.

Social pressure not only obliges individuals to respect family solidarity, but operates in a wider context. The most important and most pervasive remains that of the village. Most settlements with a tradition of emigration have seen their overseas sons come together to form village associations, by hostel, by town, even for the whole of France. Each village association has a firm, organised structure, with a president, assisted by a committee, which includes both a secretary and a treasurer. The Soninke, in particular, show a remarkable propensity to form associations (by age-group, by neighbourhood, around a particular project), whose structure is always marked by a great formalism. The common denominator of most of these institutions[13] is that they are generally organised around a 'fund', supplied by members' subscriptions and with clearly defined objectives. Most commonly, these funds are used for mutual-aid purposes and for 'emergencies' in cases of immediate need (sickness, unemployment, reception of a newly-arrived migrant). They can also be used as loans to young men coming to France for the first time. Between these communities and their villages or origins the links remain very close. Several thousands of kilometres away, in the heart of a large industrial city, many migrants continue to live by the same customs as they did in their home villages. This is not a matter of individual psychology, but a social phenomenon deliberately encouraged and maintained by the traditional authorities concerned. Thus it is not uncommon for a 'marabout' or an emissary from the head of a village to spend several weeks or months in France, visiting the hostels where migrants from his village are grouped. This control obviously has its economic functions. Thus, these 'tours' are often made at a time when a collection is launched for a village project, usually the building of a mosque, but also, as in Diaguili, that of a dispensary.[14] It is no exaggeration to say that in such projects we are witnessing the emergence of a form of 'collective village budget'. Certainly there is a big difference between the construction of a building for collective use, and the implementation of activities likely to have profound repercussions on the economic life of the community (in the form of exacerbating rivalries and competition between individuals). However, there are some signs that significant changes are taking place in this domain. Diaguili has recently established a consumers' co-operative dealing in everyday consumable goods, the members of which are planning to use a part of the collective savings to augment its capital. Some villages have large sums in reserve (several hundreds of thousands of Ouguiyas) which they intend to use for some activity of collective benefit, although they are still not sure of the best way to use them. Sometimes they find a specific project, as in the case of

Bouanze, where the young men bought two motor pumps (now out of use) to equip the village well.

As we have seen, workers living in France are subject to multiple pressures (from the family environment, the village community, mutual-aid societies), which are designed to recover the major part of the money they earn. None the less, whatever the strength of these demands, there are many, among the elders in particular, who endeavour to maintain personal control over the greater part of the savings that they manage to accrue. We find the most obvious expression of this desire in the institution of 'men of confidence' (*duntegne*) — retired civil servants, former migrants and, above all, traders, whose role is to receive, look after and manage the money sent by the migrants. There are different types of *duntegne*, from the man who undertakes to cash the money-orders for a few personal friends, to the rich trader who has several million Ouguiyas passing through his hands. In certain cases we can see the beginnings of a banking institution. The migrants make the deposits with their 'man of confidence', who in turn uses the money for personal speculations.[15]

In fact, these practices illustrate an obvious desire to evade the economic pressures of society, and to keep some control over the use of money sent home. When a migrant makes out a money-order, he usually writes out on the counterfoil the use he would like to see made of it. According to the information that we have gathered, only a part is destined for the family. The rest goes to swell his personal savings (*dundukhuma*). This fact is rarely mentioned in the few studies of this problem and should be underlined, because it is extremely significant from the point of view of the function of emigration within local socio-economic structures. In fact it shows that, over and above the social cohesion and communal organisation which it engenders, in the final analysis migration constitutes an activity undertaken in the pursuit of private ends.

As far as the actual use of money is concerned, the distinction between sums remitted by the migrants to their family, and the sums which they reserve for their own use, is also important.

The money received by the families is essentially directed towards daily subsistence expenses, as well as to recurrent expenses: food, upkeep of houses and, until recently, payment of taxes. We shall return to the question of food later, but we can mention in passing that in those villages where migration is sizeable and long-established, eating habits have been considerably modified. Rice is gradually replacing millet, particularly for the midday meal; the consumption of bread is more and more common; and the use of expensive imported goods such as groundnut oil, tinned milk, instant coffee, sugar and tomato sauce has become commonplace. As a corollary to the stagnation or even regression of local agricultural production, we can see a growing dependence by the subsistence sector on imported goods. The depletion of the available work force of each family is a partial explanation of this process. It is useful to note, however, that a share of the money sent home (often a large one) is used to take on hired labourers during the rainy season.

How the money is used is largely the responsibility of the head of the family remaining at home. In many cases, however, the migrant makes it clear to his 'man of confidence' what amounts he wants to be given directly to such and such a person. In this way, he tries to ensure that his mother, his wives, or a particular brother or sister who has called on his help will actually get the money he wishes to give them. To a degree varying from family to family, migrants are trying to exercise control, even from a distance, over the use which is made of their money. The power of the traditional hierarchy, in which the elders occupy a dominant place, is less and less able to withstand the individual aspirations of the young (among whom the majority of migrants are recruited).

As for the share of personal savings which the absentee wishes to keep for himself, it can be held, at least partially, in the form of cash by the *duntegne*. Frequently, it is 'invested' in the form of cattle. These are then added to the family herd, although their individual ownership is clearly established and understood. Over the last decade, the herds of the Soninke farmers have grown considerably. Although inquiries about the number of cattle are generally received with a fair degree of suspicion, a number of Soninke villages can reasonably be supposed to have more than a thousand head of cattle at the present time.

Although, in its various forms, this personal saving constitutes to a large extent an 'investment' for future security (that can be used in unforeseen emergencies), it also provides the means for deferred consumption. Indeed, on his return the migrant often lavishly spends the sums accumulated in his absence.

Firstly, there are many bachelors whose reason for their first departure to France is to accumulate the money they will need to pay for their marriage (a responsibility which formerly fell on the head of the family).[16] Marriage is a very expensive undertaking, sometimes involving an outlay of tens of thousands of Ouguiyas, as well as one or several head of cattle. Initially, there are a number of institutionally imposed obligations:

the *tama*: an 'engagement' present, marking reciprocal

commitment of the two families: traditionally made up of kola nuts and cloth.

the *futte*: a dowry given to the woman on marriage: one or several cows, or their equivalent in money.

the *nabure*: given to the male relatives of the bride; kola nuts and a large sum of money (often more than 15,000 Ouguiyas).

But in addition there are other presents less formally prescribed, a series which begins before the 'engagement' and continues up to the marriage itself: presents given every year to the young woman and her relatives at each religious festival; the bride's 'trousseau', including clothes, jewels, perfume and, more recently, a tape-recorder, a radio, a sewing machine. It is with all these optional gifts that competition between suitors reaches its height, by 'raising the bidding' and sometimes leading to disproportionate expense. We have heard of some marriages costing more than 100,000 Ouguiyas.

Moreover, on his return the migrant will undertake new building or improvements to his personal dwelling. Refacing the walls with cement, or covering the roof with corrugated iron, can raise the cost considerably (to 100,000 Ouguiyas or even more). As is frequently the case, even if the house is in the middle of the family compound, this form of expenditure is normally provided by the occupant alone. One might ask whether these alterations represent a true improvement in living conditions, particularly the corrugated iron roofs, which are extremely uncomfortable in the hot season. What is certain, however, is that they meet an obvious desire to lessen maintenance work during the long absence of the head of the household.

There are also purchases of furniture: deckchairs, armchairs, mattresses, mosquito-nets etc., some of which they bring back from France, but quite a lot of which they buy en route in Nouakchott or Dakar. Clothes are another important category on which savings are spent: 'pagnes' (a length of cloth worn sarong-style) for wives; shirts, shorts and shoes for the children; large 'boubous' and traditional trousers for men, etc. We know of one man who spent more than 20,000 Ouguiyas on clothes.

The gold jewellery that the women wear has a special role here, that of a valuable reserve. It usually consists of rings and pendants worn in the ear. Often young girls wear in their hair thin bands of leather or cloth decorated with little rings of gold. Thus, small fortunes, sometimes as much as 50 grammes of gold per ear, are to be seen worn in the street. According to our information, which should be checked with the women concerned, this jewellery represents a sort of 'deposit' entrusted by a husband to his wives.

He retains the right to reclaim them in the case of separation or even of dire need.

When the migrant returns home after a long absence, he is expected to display great generosity. Not only must he give many small presents to those around him, and refuse help to none who ask, but he must also ensure that for his family and friends his return is marked by a period of festivity and plenty. This is why he often returns with sacks of rice, barrels of vegetable oil, packets of sugar, condensed milk and instant coffee, and keeps open house for several weeks.

To sum up our observations on the distribution and use of money arising from emigration, we think it is important to stress a certain number of points.

(i) We must remember first of all that migrants control a considerable part of their income, except the more junior, who are entirely controlled by their elders. Apart from personal expenses, which are often high, as we have just seen, they are obviously anxious to accumulate some savings for future security. This most frequently takes the form of cattle, although it is increasingly becoming oriented towards the 'modern' sectors: land speculation, and investment in new buildings in the new districts of the large cities.

(ii) Although the effect of migration on material living conditions is noticeable (food, housing, etc.), the tendency to immediate consumption is on the whole restrained. To a large extent, the Soninke and Toucouleur remain masters of the money they handle, in contrast to other parts of Africa affected by the colonial barter economy. In these latter regions, the deliberate policy of incitement to over-consumption through the creation of debts, carried out by the commercial houses and their intermediaries, has created the situation of a forced circulation of cash and the constant 'race' after money (Raynaut, 1977). This is undoubtedly one of the advantages of the isolation of the Guidimaka over this last half-century. However great the growing intensity of its dependence on the exterior (particularly worrying in the case of food), the situation is still a far cry from the large-scale dependency of the peasants of the groundnut-producing regions. The maintenance of a relatively solid subsistence sector, at least for basic cereals such as millet and sorghum, as well as the absence of indebtedness, leaves the Guidimakan farmers with much larger room for manoeuvre.

(iii) A last important point, linked to the preceding one, concerns the capacity of these communities to successfully undertake collective projects. It has often been regretted that the most important large investments carried out with migrants' money have usually been the building of mosques, an undertaking judged economically 'non-profitable'. On the other hand, however, we tend to see this as an important and positive act. Notwithstanding its religious meaning, it expresses the will of the village community to assert their cohesiveness and solidarity as a group. The discussions we have had with village notables and members of migrants' associations have shown that they were, in many cases, very much aware of the community dimension of their problems. As we have already mentioned, many migrants' associations have large sums of money set aside for 'village development'. In the areas at the foot of the Assaba massif, at their own initiative, the villagers have undertaken minor works to open up new land for cultivation (branch and mud dams at Ndieo). The general impression that we gained from discussions on this point was that positive proposals, backed up by the necessary technical support, would find the inhabitants of most villages ready and willing to participate. Despite this, it would be injudicious to overestimate the capacity or willingness of the Soninke to eschew personal benefits for a collective goal. The need to maintain cohesiveness could to a certain extent be seen as a conjunctural response to the problems of emigration. Only a soundly based collective organisation can enable them to take the risks and overcome the difficulties that are involved. The ultimate aim would none the less seem to be the search for individual benefit. Any attempt to transpose already existing forms of solidarity into the field of agricultural production must take account of this fact.

In concluding these remarks on the problem of emigration, an important question remains: that of its obvious impact on the system of agricultural production. There has been no introduction of new techniques. Some rare attempts have indeed been made by some migrants to bring back motor-cultivators or motor-pumps, but these experiments have almost all failed. The very unskilled work undertaken by migrants in France gives them no form of training that they could use on their return. The few chances they will have had to observe other agricultural practices on their travels are obviously of no help with the problems they find on returning to their villages.

Such changes as there have been in agriculture have been retrogressive rather than progressive. To illustrate this, however, an overall analysis of the agricultural production system is required. This is what we shall attempt in the following pages.

NOTES

1 Estimate made in the villages on both sides of the river : the Mauritanian and Senegalese banks.
2 Dubresson (op.cit.) gives an even higher frequency: 'We have calculated that on average an African worker stayed 3 months in the same job, and then changed.'
3 Doubtless 1971, but they do not give a date.
4 About £3,200,000.
5 About £750,000.
6 About £445.
7 Which also corresponds to calculations made in France on the basis of an average monthly income of 900 FF and a savings rate of 40 per cent.
8 About £1,700,000.
9 Approx. £1,170,000.
10 Particularly because we are completely unaware of the real number of migrants who conform effectively to the 'norm'. The young would seem increasingly to wish to assert their independence: this often takes the form of failure to fulfill the obligation to send money.
11 'According to a note from the "Commissariat au Plan" (in France), there are 1.8 per cent work accidents per month amongst Africans. This is a record compared to figures for other nationalities, and also, a fortiori, compared to the French population.' (IDEP, 1972, p.88).
12 'From the family to the village, from the village to the "Cercle", from the "Cercle" to the region, a living image of the river valley is thus reproduced.' (Dubresson, op.cit., p.20.)
13 Some of which, particularly those organised round age-groups, correspond to long-established forms of organisation.
14 Although one does not see, on the Mauritanian bank, the blossoming of grandiose mosques that one sees in the Senegalese villages!
15 There are cases, admittedly rare, of *duntegne* going 'bankrupt'; becoming unable to reimburse depositors when they demand it. An interesting question, which we cannot answer, is whether 'men of confidence' have a role (advisors, consultants, middlemen) in the current direction of some migrants' savings towards large-scale speculations: property speculation in the cities, particularly.
16 This underlines the point that emigration is an attempt, at an individual level, to mitigate the breakdown of the traditional system of production and of distribution of wealth.

SECTION B

AN OUTLINE ANALYSIS OF THE AGRICULTURAL PRODUCTION SYSTEM

In discussing this topic, we shall consider the process of agricultural production as occurring within a system which incorporates environmental, technological and social factors linked together by identifiable and relatively stable relationships.

Of course, we are not in a position to elucidate such a system in its entirety after such a rapid initial survey. However, while remaining at a level of generalisation, we are able to emphasise particularly important relationships and to indicate in which evolutionary directions they occur. It is clear that within this approach we shall give particular attention to the phenomenon of migration as an important element of change.

CHAPTER 8

The Structure and Functioning of the Physical Environment

The physical environment in this context refers to the geographical areas surrounding the villages in the Guidimaka and which either affect the lives of the villagers in various ways, or are exploited by them. Thus, we are concerned with the interaction between geographical space and human activity. In terms of this exploitation this space can be divided into a number of land systems within which are found the different cultivated lands of the region and through which their organisation and functioning can be comprehended. It is from this viewpoint that we now discuss the physical environment.

I A COMPLEX LAND SYSTEM OFFERING A WIDE RANGE OF POSSIBILITIES

It seems possible to divide the land system, on the basis of the natural differences that determine the form of organisation of the lands, into two major categories corresponding to the two geographical zones to which we have already drawn attention: the riverine and interior zones.

1. *The Riverine Lands*

These lands are very similar to those which have been described and analysed previously in studies of the Senegal valley (Boutillier and Cantrelle, 1962; Papy, 1951) and in studies of particular villages (Le Blanc, 1962; Ravault, 1964).

As everywhere along the river, a fundamental distinction can be drawn between the flood plain and the higher land; between flood-retreat agriculture and dry-land farming. This division is revealed in the following land types:

(a) *The* falo
This is the bank of the river. The highest point in the bank is known as the *falo* and has sandy soils. The lowest point and the last to emerge from the retreating flood is called the *wuso* and has a sandy clay soil. The following crops are grown in rows running parallel to the river and are sown in stages as the river falls: sorghum, cowpeas, tomatoes, pumpkins, calabashes and sweet potatoes.

(b) *The* fonde
This is the large alluvial levee of the river. Its higher parts (*fonde ranere*) are rarely flooded and have a sandy or silty-sandy soil. Sorghum and millet are usually grown here, occasionally with groundnuts. The lower part of the *fonde* (*fonde wallere* or *fonde noir*) may be flooded in years of high discharge. Its soil contains slightly more clay and is more fertile. These areas are particularly well suited to the rain-fed cultivation of maize and sorghum, alone or in association with cowpeas. There are also some small areas where perennial indigo, okra, cotton and calabashes are grown. Continuing down the slope, away from the river, cultivated areas tend to give way to bush as flooding is more and more frequent, even during normal years, causing damage to rain-fed crops. Despite this high frequency of occurrence, the flood is inadequate for flood-retreat cultivation.

(c) *The* walo

In this zone a major division is noticeable. First is the *hollalde wallere* or *hollalde noir*, the lowest lying area whose soil contains the most clay. This area is sown as late as possible with long-cycle (more than 120 days) varieties of sorghum. In deeper depressions, small plots of rice may be grown. Second is the *hollalde ranere* or *hollalde blanc*, which is higher up and exposed earlier after the flood. It has a less clayey soil, which is suitable for the cultivation of maize and shorter-cycle (less than 120 days) varieties of sorghum.

(d) *The* dieri

Two major soil types may be identified. First there is the *signa*, a sandy soil which is normally devoted to millet and groundnuts; and secondly, the *katamagne*, with more clay and which is usually sown with short-cycle sorghum. Reference to Figure 6 indicates the juxta-position of these zones.

These large and relatively homogeneous areas are only exploited in a relatively extensive manner. However, there are some small, enclosed areas on the *fonde*, near to the villages, which are used as cattle pens in the dry season, when they are comprehensively manured. There, maize and short-cycle sorghum are more intensively cultivated in the rainy season.

The distribution of crop types across these soil systems is illustrated in more detail in Table IX.

Thus we see that the riverine land system is made up of numerous distinct areas, each of which is defined by particular environmental conditions and a particular agricultural specialisation. We shall try to show later how these different elements are articulated in time and space to form a relatively cohesive agricultural production system. It is obvious, however, that if there is any change in the balance between the different lands, particularly in terms of their area or location in relation to the village, then what is actually changed is the balance within the total system. Thus, Diaguili is characterised by the existence of an extensive area of good quality *dieri* close to the village. The production of millet and groundnuts is therefore of an importance that is not always found elsewhere. At Diogountourou, on the other hand, one of the features is the size and quality of the *fonde*, which is suitable for maize, and here the farmers give special importance to this crop. In the village of Mouderi on the Senegalese side of the river, the *fonde* is a relatively small area and the *dieri* is a long way from the village, but there are very large depressions which are cultivated in flood-retreat.

It may be said in conclusion that, on the basis of the general

Table IX

Distribution of crops and varieties according to zones of cultivation

Crops	Varieties	Cycle	Yield*	Zones of Cultivation Interior	River
Sorghum — loose panicle (Fela)	Mangagne Badiabale	210 days	–	lower Rakhe	Walo hollalde
	White Fela	120/150 days	800 kg/ha	Rakhe/Paraole	Walo Walere/Fonde Walere
	Nebane Leme	90 days	1.040 kg/ha	Paraole/Katamagne	Fonde Walere/Katamagne
Sorghum — dense panicle (Nienco)	Khore Maundo	120/150 days	1.700 kg/ha	Rakhe/Paraole	Walo Walere/Fonde Walere
	Sidi nieliba	80/90 days	850 kg/ha	Paraole/Katamagne	Fonde Walere/Katamagne
	Sie tombe Sili maya	70 days	–	Paraole/Katamagne	Fonde Walere
	Samba dieri	90 days	640 kg/ha	Dieri signa	Dieri signa
Millet Pennisetum	Suna	80/90 days	640 kg/ha	Dieri signa	Dieri signa
	Sagno	120 days	–	Katamagne/Paraole	Fonde ranere/Katamagne
Cowpeas (niebe)	Mise	90 days	–	Rakhe/Paraole	FondeWalere/Falo
	?	180 days	–	Rakhe bas	–

Crop	Variety	Duration	Yield		
Maize	Dumbe	90 days	–	Paraole cattle pens	Walo walere/Fonde walere cattle pens
	?	120 days	–	Rakhe	Walo walere/Fonde walere Falo
Groundnut	Tiga sasa	90 days	590 kg/ha	Dieri signa	Dieri signa/Fonde ranere
	Tiga fune	120 days	–	Dieri signa/Katamagne	Fonde ranere/Dieri signa
Rice	Maro sinisire	100 days	–	Rakhe flooded	Collengal –
	Maro kas barene	120 days	–	Rakhe flooded	–
	Maro khore	150 days	–	deeply flooded depressions	deeply flooded depressions
Potatoes	–	120/150 days	–	Falo (rare)	Falo
Calabashes	–	100/120 days	–	Paraole	Fonde walere/Falo
Gombo (ladies' fingers)	–	90 days	–	Paraole	Fonde walere/Falo

*These yield figures are provided only as an indication of size. They were obtained on trial plots of the Secteur Agricole of Selibabi.

N.B. in the text the spelling *walere* and *wallere* are used interchangeably picture that we have given above, there are as many patterns of use of the different lands as there are villages. Each one is characterised by its own special balance between zones with different uses, and consequently by its own different orientation being given to the system of agricultural production.

2. The Lands of the Interior

In the interior of the Guidimaka, around the villages on the edge of the dry valleys of the Garfa and the Niorde, the organisation of the agricultural lands changes profoundly. The flood zones of the *walo* and the *falo* disappear almost completely, or are only a very small part of the available land.[1] Instead we find expanses of low-lying land (*rakhe*) beside the marigots. These are flooded when the streams overflow, but they do not receive sufficient water to permit cultivation as the flood recedes (see Figure 6). The slopes of the depressions (*paraole*) are sometimes cultivated (increasingly, as we shall see later). The really low-lying lands are sown with long-cycle sorghum, the slopes with short-cycle varieties and with maize.

Here also the second main component of the land system is the *dieri*. This is put to the same use as in the riverine zones.

Emerging from this schema are two essential features which should be stressed.

(i) The range of agricultural possibilities is considerably smaller than in the riverine villages. Only dry-land farming is possible on a large scale. Except in a few small areas, cultivation is difficult in the dry season without irrigation. A few examples of irrigation have been found: in Dafort, where there is a tradition of tobacco growing,[2] at Bouanze, where we found an orchard of some years' standing, with mangoes, lemons, guavas, pawpaws, dates and henna; and, finally, at Ajar and Hassi-Chaggar. It should also be noted that the Agricultural Services at Selibabi carried out a useful exercise in 1973-75 (within the framework of a plan covering the whole of the Third Region), in distributing equipment and seeds to encourage vegetable gardening. Although this initiative aroused a lively interest among the farmers, it was not followed through in 1974/75 because of a lack of seed and anti-acridian insecticide. Most of these gardens have now been abandoned.

(ii) The fragmentation of lands into cultivated zones which are widely dispersed throughout extensive areas of uncultivated land. Instead of these being a relatively regular succession of more or less parallel strips, as there is beside the river, the depressions which are cultivated in the interior areas are distributed according to the irregular topography, in what is often a very wide area around a village. We quote the examples of Harr, which has an area of *rakhe* 8 km. to the north-east of the village, an area of *paraole* the same distance to the south, and another depression which is a little nearer the village but to the west. Even if this phenomenon is not quite so pronounced in all villages, the general situation is the same throughout, to the extent that the time spent travelling to the fields presents a special problem, particularly in view of the fact that the agricultural calendar is so tight.

In addition to these characteristics, which are common to all the villages of the interior, the diversity which we have already noted in the context of the riverine villages is also evident. Each village is situated at the heart of its original lands, with its own specific features, both positive and negative. At Harr it is the proximity of the sandy *dieri* which surrounds the village, in contrast to the distance of the cultivated depressions we referred to in the preceding paragraph. At Ndieo it is the presence of a string of temporary lakes at the foot of the Assaba escarpment, which allows the large-scale cultivation of rice. This village is therefore largely self-sufficient in this cereal but, on the other hand, suffers from a lack of *rakhe* land suitable for sorghum cultivation. Oulombome has an area of *walo* large enough for each family to cultivate at least one field in flood-retreat, but it has only a small area suitable for rice.

Perhaps even more so than along the river, there is in the interior a marked diversity between the villages. Each situation deserves individual analysis to isolate and identify its dominant features. This task is not possible within this brief overview, but the existence of such diversity is a factor whch needs to be emphasised.

II   THE ARTICULATION BETWEEN THE DIFFERENT ZONES OF THE AGRICULTURAL LAND SYSTEM

As we have seen above, the different zones and their use are articulated in space and time to form a whole whose components are closely interdependent.

1. *In space*

It may be said that the present organisation of the land system indicates an attempt to draw the maximum possible advantage from the potential of the natural environment, given the knowledge and technical means available. This aspect of the situation may be considered both from a static point of view (the use made of the space at a given point in time), and through its dynamics (the changes which land use undergoes as a function of modification of particular factors in the general situation).

From a static point of view (as if one were to take a photograph of the distribution of the different areas of cultivated land at a given moment), it may be seen that the Soninke and Toucouleur farmers exploit the diversity of their natural environment in a remarkable manner. They manage to do so through a precise knowledge of soils and of the potential and requirements of the different crop varieties which they have been able to select. Table IX, 'Crop varieties and their distribution across the different land systems of the Guidimaka', provides an illustration of this adaptation between crop varieties and soil types.[2]

We believe that, given the crop varieties which are known and the techniques at their disposal, the farmers of the Guidimaka are at present making optimal use of their environment. Any attempt to improve agricultural production must take this diversity as its starting point and not tend to reduce it. On the contrary, through the introduction of new crops, varieties and techniques, such attempts must try to widen the range of crops and to make possible the use of parts of the land which are now used incompletely or not at all.[3]

From a dynamic point of view, it is clear that the concrete conditions for the use of space are largely dependent on variable external factors such as rainfall and the height and duration of the flood. However, the farmers are not passive in the face of such uncertainties. In fact, they are able to modify their use of the space available to them to meet any given situation, and in some cases they even make provisions beforehand for the different foreseeable possibilities. Such behaviour was particularly evident during the period of drought which has just ended. The areas near the river, which are flooded in years of high flood, were sown at the beginning of the rainy season with sorghum or rice. So long as the flooding was slight, these plots could be dry-farmed like the *rakhe* of the interior. If the flood was as normal, these same areas would be completely inundated, and the crops destroyed. Flood-retreat agriculture then became possible, however.

Elsewhere the lower part of the *fonde*, which is not cultivable in a normal year, has been widely cleared and cultivated during recent years of drought. In the villages where the *fonde* zones cover a larger area than the *walo* (such as Diogountourou), the use of the latter would tend to play a kind of supplementary role. In the rainy season, the farmers cultivate the largest area of *fonde* which is possible (given the work-force available, and the quality of the land they can use). If the flood is high there is a calendar problem, since it will recede late and there will be competition between harvesting the *fonde* fields on the one hand and the preparing of soil and the sowing of the *walo* on the other. In such a case, the farmers limit the areas worked on the *walo* to the amount which they consider necessary to supplement their crop from the *fonde*.

In the villages of the interior there is less margin for manoeuvre. None the less, here too the farmers do what they can to protect themselves from the vagaries of the rainfall. To do this they first of all take care to sow within the same zone varieties with different growth cycles, so as to ensure a reasonable average yield whatever happens. When a longer-term tendency becomes discernible, as in recent years, they gradually switch their preference to the crops and varieties which are most resistant. Thus we have seen a substantial withdrawal from groundnuts and from long-cycle pennisetum millet (*sagno*).

It should also be noted that there is a general tendency in the region as a whole towards a partial abandonment of the *dieri*, either in favour of the slopes of the basins (*paraole*), or in the river villages in favour of the lower part of the *fonde*.

Other factors may intervene in the choice of the use of the different areas. In particular are the complementary or competitive relationships which arise between agriculture and animal husbandry. Thus, the farmers of Diaguili are able to cultivate maize on certain parts of their *dieri* with the manure from the Peul cattle which are kept at times on their land. On the other hand, some of the basins near to Sangue-Dieri village have had to be abandoned because of damage done by cattle.

Thus, as we can see from these different examples, there is great flexibility in the use of the natural environment. None the less, the dynamics of this process always operate towards attenuating the unforeseen variations in natural factors in such a way as to maintain the overall coherence of the system.

It appears that, under these conditions, any attempt to change, even partially, such a system must try either to preserve the existing balance or to substitute for it a new and lasting equilibrium.

2. *In time*

The time factor is particularly important from the point of view of the overall coherence of the agrarian system. It can be analysed from two points of view: that of the articulation of agricultural operations, and that of the staggering of the harvests, and therefore of the supply of food products.

(a) *The agricultural calendar*

Here again, we must distinguish between the cultivated land beside the river and that of the interior. As may be seen from Figure 10, in the villages beside the river there are three points where there is clear competition between the activities undertaken in the different zones of land.

First of all, we note the overall competition between the cultivation of the *dieri* and that of the *fonde*. This is particularly noticeable at the beginning of the rainy season, when the sowing of sorghum and maize on the *fonde* coincides with the beginning of the weeding of the millet, sorghum and maize in the *dieri*. Any delay in carrying out either of these operations could have serious consequences for the corresponding harvests. We see then that the farmers are forced to make a choice on the basis of the work-force at their disposal, and to find some balance between the areas cultivated on the *dieri* and those cultivated on the *fonde*.[4] In this respect, the greater or lesser distance of the *dieri* from the village, as well as the drain on manpower through migration, constitute large impediments.

The second bottleneck occurs, in a year of normal flooding, between the harvesting of the dry-farmed crops and the sowing of the flood-retreat fields. Here again, any delay to either operation could have disastrous results and, as we stressed above, this competition tends to be resolved in favour of the *fonde* in those villages where this provides the farmers with the most important part of their resources.

A third type of competition is to be found between farming on the *walo* and on the *falo*. As can be seen from Figure 10, these tend to overlap in time. It should be noted, however, that the *falo* is generally only a relatively small part of the village agricultural land and, also, that it is generally monopolised by a small number of families who have access to its use.

In the villages of the interior the land available generally offers a much narrower range of possibilities. Thus, with a few exceptions, the whole range of agricultural tasks is concentrated in the rainy season (see Figure 10). Consequently, there is overall competition between the farming on the *dieri* and that in the depressions (*rakhe*) or on their slopes (*paraole*). Once again, it is difficult to reconcile the two coincident tasks of sowing in the *rakhe* and weeding on the *dieri*. Furthermore, there is a complicating factor; namely, the fragmentation of the lands which we noted above, which makes the journeys between the different zones of cultivated land very time-consuming.

At the end of the rainy season (late September) there is a second

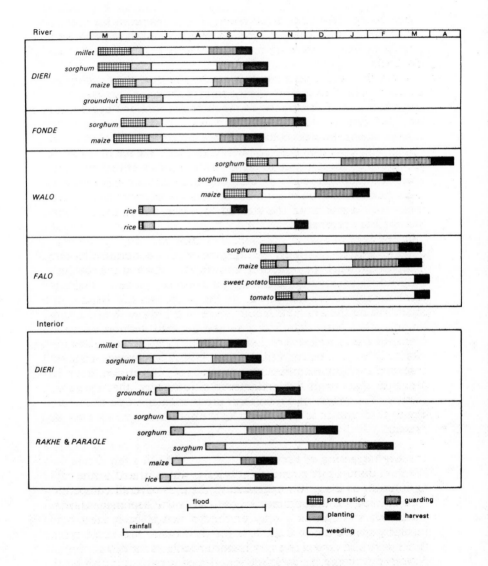

Fig. 10 Calendar of agricultural activities in the different zones of the riverine and land systems

bottleneck, when it becomes necessary to undertake simultaneously the harvesting of maize and *suna* and the weeding of the fields on the *rakhe*.

Finally, in October and November, the preparation for sowing the longer-cycle sorghum (in the lowest-lying land) competes with guarding of the medium-cycle varieties (sown on the slopes) from predators.

From this very rapid analysis it can be seen that the Guidimaka farmers must achieve a very delicate balance between the requirements and constraints of the different forms of agriculture that they practise. One method of doing this is by adjusting the relative size of the areas cultivated in the different zones of the land system which occur in the riverine villages, and is made possible by the variety of choices open to them within a relatively concentrated area. Another method is by adapting their agricultural calendar according to the growth-cycle of the varieties of crops which they use, which seems more the method to which the farmers of the interior have recourse.

In the face of such a situation, it is clear that any agricultural development project must be designed with strict regard to the complex network of temporal constraints which we have just outlined. In each village this takes on a specific pattern, resulting most notably from the layout of the land and the impact of migration on the available labour force. No project should begin on any other basis than a precise and detailed analysis of these elements, made in close association with the farmers themselves.[5] Not only must it be ensured that any innovations which may be contemplated will not create new situations of competition, but it is also clear that one of the fundamental objectives of any project to improve the system of agricultural production must be above all else to eliminate or at least attenuate the bottlenecks which exist at present.

(b) *The staggering of harvests*

We shall discuss this second point briefly, which is not in any way to diminish its essential importance in the eyes of the farmers. By their choice of appropriate crops and varieties, the farmers endeavour to obtain a supply of food which is both early and regularly spaced out in time. It is for this reason that short-cycle rice, maize and *suna* play a very important role as 'bridging' crops. Next in time come the different varieties of sorghum, grown both by dry-farming and in flood-retreat, which are harvested from the end of September until April (beside the river), and from the end of September until January/February (in the interior). The gap between the last harvest of one year and the first of the next is thus five months in the first case and nine months in the second.

These comments are intended to underline an aspect of the farmers' normal practice which plays an essential part in securing their food supply. Any project to bring about agricultural changes must necessarily take account of it, particularly if it is seeking to make improvements in this regard.

NOTES

1 There is, in particular, some *walo* at Harr, Ajar, Oulombome and some *falo* at Ajar, on the banks of the Oued Garfa.
2 It should be noted that the farmers' search for new varieties is still continuing: thus the sorghum variety *Sidi nieliba* was very recently introduced and its use spread rapidly during the drought.
3 For example, some of the soils around Ndieo seem to be under-used from the point of view of their *physical* qualities. It is possible that there are social and economic constraints which limit their use.
4 For example, some zones of good-quality soil have been studied on the inner edge of the *walo*, 5 km. to the west of Golmi. It is possible that this land is not utilised at present because of its distance from the village, or of competition for the work-force. In the same way, some alternative land, with good-quality soil, is available at Ndiao.
5 The question of the availability of alternative cultivable lands and the selection of these in the framework of a development project, demands an in-depth study at the level of each village. At the moment, it seems that there may be alternatives from the point of view of physical resources, given that socio-economic restraints will be determinant.

CHAPTER 9

Environmental Dynamics and the Current Evolution of the Village Land Systems

We have just described the spatial organisation of the land systems of the zone studied, and analysed the manner in which their constituent elements are articulated in space and time so as to constitute, at a technical level, coherent agrarian systems. These systems, as we have seen, are dynamic and are constantly adapting to the environmental conditions in which they exist.

There are two areas within which variations are particularly important. Firstly, there are the facts of the physical environment, which have undergone a major disturbance in these last years of drought. Secondly, there are social and economic conditions which affect the technical behaviour adopted by human groups in exploiting the resources of the natural environment they live in.

It is these two aspects that we shall examine now.

I THE DROUGHT AND THE DISTURBANCE OF THE NATURAL ENVIRONMENT

The most spectacular environmental upset in recent years has been the drought of the late 1960s and early 1970s. Although there is no doubt that this latest drought was severe in both its magnitude and its duration, it should be acknowledged that rainfall in the West African dry savannah zone is typically highly variable. The concept of average rainfall in this context is of limited practicality. By any definition, dry years are frequent in occurrence, and cause little comment. In this particular instance, the *succession of several very dry years*, and the world-wide coverage in the media, have heightened awareness of what is otherwise just another element of risk to agriculture in the Sahel. Furthermore, as we noted in the Introduction, the annual variation which is evident in the figures is probably of secondary importance to local agriculture when compared with the effectiveness of the rains, and their known variability from place to place, over very short distances.

As far as the effect (lasting or otherwise) of the drought on the prevailing environmental dynamics is concerned, we shall concentrate on two areas: firstly vegetation and then soils and erosion.

1. *Vegetation*

It has been suggested in various papers and articles that the drought has been responsible (or will be responsible) for massive, wide-scale deterioration of the vegetal cover of the Sahelian zone. Specifically, the broad-scale death of trees, the permanent loss of grass cover[1] and, as a result, exposure of the soil to wind erosion, would lead to a progressive southward movement of the desert. The exact meaning of the last phrase need not be discussed for the moment, though the implications are clear. Set against this forecast, it must be emphasised that the position of the Soninke lands is in the southern transitional zone of the Sahel, and therefore unlikely to suffer the extremes of desert advance. On a more local scale, it is possible to conceive of areas of sandy soil, prone to rapid dessication, and in severely restricted rainfall, subject to a decline in vegetal ground cover.

Such a condition might lead to either wind-blown soil erosion, or, at the onset of heavy rains, sheetwash erosion and subsequent gullying. Evidence of such environmental degradation is found in the densely peopled areas of Northern Nigeria and Southern Niger, but is due as much to over-intensive usage as to inadequate rainfall. In the region studied, only localised and limited signs of the effect of the drought upon the vegetation have been seen. Several dead trees were observed at Harr and south of Ndieo, and on the edge of the *dieri* to the west of Bakel, but within these areas such occurrences were exceptional rather than commonplace. In addition, in certain of the *dieri* areas more fundamental changes in vegetation were observed. In particular, on the lateritic areas east of Selibabi and on some of the sand-dune systems between Gouraye and Selibabi, expanses of dead trees were noted. However, there appears to have been a selective mortality of trees. In particular, *Pterocarpus lucens* seems to have suffered the most. Large stands of these trees were observed to have died, presumably as a result of the drought, but alongside them specimens of *Combretum glutinosum, Sterculia setigera* and *Guiera senegalensis* (the last in contrast to the findings at Fete Ole (shown by Poupon and Bille, 1974)) seem to have survived without obvious damage. On the sand system immediately north of Gouraye, large areas of damaged and dead *Combretum glutinosum* are attributed to an extensive fire in the spring of 1975 which may have been a contributary factor after the difficulties experienced during the drought. Where such widespread mortality was observed newly initiated, minor erosion channels were apparent. However, it is probable that with several seasons' good rain, regenerating shrub communities and the development of a better grass cover will protect these otherwise fairly stable terrain forms. Such incidence of incipient erosion would seem to be as much a function of human action as of the problems experienced during the drought and immediately after. Where erosion was observed the localities coincided with agricultural activity or with tracks which are used for animal seasonal migration. Where such human action is less apparent the savannas of the region were, by contrast, remarkable for their density, their height and the general vigour of the trees. Similarly, there was no clear evidence of a widespread decline in grass cover. Again, as with the tree cover, large areas supported dense and vigorous grassland. Although detailed examination was not possible, the dominant genera appeared to be *Andropogon* and *Hyparrhenia*, perennially tufted grasses whose rootstocks must have survived the dry years if seeds were not available. Annual species of *Chloris, Aristida*, and *Eragrostis* were also encountered, however. With reference to the possible loss of annual species through failing seed viability during the drought, it is important to acknowledge that there was never a complete absence of rain. During the drought the minimum annual total recorded from Bakel was 369 mm. in 1972, more than adequate to support such annual species as *Schoenfeldia gracilis* and *Eragrostis tremula*, which normally tolerate the much lower precipitation of the more northern Sahel. As a generalisation, an observer would have difficulty discerning evidence of drought from undisturbed vegetation within the region.

Rather surprisingly, this is particularly true of the *dieri*, both on the Continental Terminal (including lateritic areas) of Senegal, and in the interior areas of Mauritania: land systems which are the driest of the region (in terms of soil moisture), have the lowest soil fertility and would therefore be expected to suffer first and most dramatically from an extended drought. The exceptions to this statement are the sand-dune systems surrounding the Assaba massif. Observations to the north and the south of Ndieo[2] indicate complete disappearance of grass cover during the dry season on the relic dunes (dating from the arid phase preceding the Nouakchottian transgression). These systems are still unconsolidated and mobile (the more extensive dunes to the east of the Assaba massif were not seen), but it is probable that, being in the north of the Soninke region, and characterised by more overtly Sahelian vegetation, this mobile state is their natural condition, with or without drought incidence. In any event, these areas are not used for agriculture or grazing, and though they may be the first to reflect deteriorating physical conditions, this need not be detrimental to local farming.

Although the *dieri* shows little evidence of natural vegetational change, the same observation cannot be made about the alluvial lands of the Senegal valley and its tributaries. This is not because natural change has not occurred, but because the effect of human activities has effectively masked it. In fact, as the *dieri* systems seem fairly stable, it is highly probable that the alluvial areas would not have suffered unduly if human interference had been less obvious. As far as the drought is concerned, the greatest impact on the physical environment has been indirect: changes induced by human action which in itself is a response to the drought. We shall return to this point later.

2. *Soils and Erosion*

Occasional references to soil erosion in the previous section stressed the protective nature of vegetation, and in particular a grass cover. Soil erosion in the arid tropics can be through wind loss or through sheetwash and gullying. At present there appears to be only a restricted incidence of erosion. Wind blow of loose surface material undoubtedly occurs in the region, though neither its frequency nor its intensity is known. The sandy areas around the Assaba massif, and the smaller hills of the Mauritianian *dieri*, are most susceptible because of their inherent dryness and fragility. However, these areas are little used and not significant to the present situation. Elsewhere, if the soils are bare, they usually carry a surface crust of fine material, or are of massive structure. These 'sealed' conditions prevent wind erosion unless the crust is broken through trampling. Tracks and routeways fall into this category, but land surfaces as a whole would seem to be relatively resistant to wind erosion.

Within the Sahelian zone, wind erosion becomes progressively less important as the wetter areas to the south are approached. The location of the Soninke region in the southern half of the Sahel suggests that surface run-off, rather than wind, is the more important agent of soil removal. Factors of importance to sheetwash and gullying are the slope of the ground, the absorption capacity of the soil, the degree of protection afforded by vegetation, the intensity and frequency of rainstorms, the state of development of the drainage net, and in this particular instance the type of flooding that occurs. From the regional viewpoint, three areas deserve consideration.

(a) *Alluvial lands of the Senegal Valley*
The alluvial lands of the Senegal valley do not appear to be suffering from soil erosion, apart from restricted areas of the *walo-dieri* margin behind Gounia, Bakel and Mouderi. For the most part the massive structure of the soil, the shallow slope angles and the nature of the flood (slow encroachment, long-period inundation and slow retreat) lead to conditions of deposition rather than erosion. The *dieri* fringe is intersected by a network of poorly integrated marigots in which there is some evidence of entrenchment and headward erosion. Gully systems are not obvious, however, and even these areas seem relatively stable at the present time. Ponding of surplus water (in the rare circumstances where infiltration rates do not match rainfall) is widespread, and this points to the inadequacy of the present drainage system for accelerating downcutting and headward erosion. These last statements refer to the *walo-dieri* fringes of the Senegal river.

(b) *The Soil of the* Dieri
Dieri soils in both Senegal and Mauritania show little evidence of erosion, though intermontane basins between Gouraye and Selibabi and further north reveal localised sheetwashing and minor channel formation. The observations suggest local transfer of material rather than complete loss, and this would seem to have continued over a long time and not to have resulted from the unique conditions created by the drought. Again, the system appears relatively stable.

(c) *The alluvial lands of the Garfa drainage system*
The alluvial areas of the Garfa and its tributaries have suffered most from the change in drainage conditions. Much of the damage seen in these areas can be attributed to the clearance of savannas by cattle herders and the changing location of the cultivation practised by the Soninke, both resulting from difficulties experienced during the drought. Of specific interest is the Dafort, Bouanze, Ndieo area. In these locations the removal of vegetation has resulted in more rapid surface run-off following rainstorms. With the loss of a protective cover over the soil, raindrop energy is dissipated in splashing, which quickly breaks up surface aggregates. This then forms a crust which subsequently acts to seal the soil surface from further infiltration.[3] The increased run-off which results has caused existing channel forms to deepen and widen, so initiating a new phase of drainage development. It is also possible that the deepening of channels, particularly the Garfa oued itself (west of Ndieo, between Dafort and Bouanze), has led to more rapid

subsurface drainage of the *paraole* lands which have recently been brought into cultivation. Associated with this channel deepening is some evidence of gullying, eroding into the *paraole* itself. This is further compounded by the migratory nature of the main channel which is a product of blockage by tree debris, a result of cutting by nomads and farmers, and the decreased coherence of the *paraole* (now practically devoid of trees). However, the slope of the land is not steep (less than five degrees) and the main channel meanders in a tortuous manner. Two subtypes may be distinguished. The first is typified by the deepened channel west of Ndieo. There, slopes are steeper, and the new, deepened channel has probably lowered the ground water table and will lead to continued erosion (unless surface run-off can be arrested) until a new equilibrium is attained. The second type, north-west of Dafort and east of Bouanze, is that of the migrating, meandering channel. This again might lead to more rapid run-off but, because of the shallow local slopes, is unlikely to possess the downcutting potential of the former type.[4] Consequently, the process of channel migration may be more easily restricted, given adequate management. In both situations, much more detailed study of the local hydrology is necessary.

The question of whether or not a new cycle of erosion has been initiated is further confused by the nature of the annual flood. Again, lack of precise knowledge prevents more than a tentative review. It does seem, however, that the flood is more rapid in its approach than that of the Senegal river, remains for a much shorter period, and finally drains away more rapidly. With the exception of small areas, the lower clay content of the *paraole* soils reinforces this appraisal. Flood conditions are less depositional, and perhaps more erosional (removing the finer sediments in suspension), than in the Senegal valley itself.

The nature of the flood and its relationship with the onset of the rains and active drainage have a wider implication. First, however, it remains to be said that there is still no real evidence of sheetwash and surface soil erosion, despite increased channel activity. Amongst the recent difficulties experienced by the farmers of these northern villages is that of a lack of soil moisture during the growing season. This inadequacy may be bound up not only with the lowered subsurface water tables due to deepened channel morphology, but also with the build-up of a coherent surface film of clay during the flood. Although it has been stated that minimal deposition of suspended load is likely to occur during the short period of the flood, the formation of a clay skin (which will later seal the soil surface) is also possible through the collapse of saturated soil aggregates. If, during the farming activity suceeding the flood, tillage does not involve wholesale break-up of the soil surface (i.e. merely the preparation of individual scrapes for the sorghum seed), subsequent rain during the latter half of the wet season will tend to run off rather than infiltrate. This would occur because of the impermeable nature of the surface clay film. The critical factor in this sequence of events is the arrival time of the flood with respect to the onset of the rains, the time of planting, and the retreat of the flood and the end of the rains. Further study of these processes, and of the more fundamental problem of drainage as a total system, is essential if the suggestion of ploughing is to be properly assessed. A brief reconnaissance has suggested that ploughing of the *paraole* will improve infiltration of rain-water. On the other hand, it might initiate more damaging surface erosion if it is practised prior to the flood, which itself may be found to be fast-flowing with a high load-carrying capacity. If the land is ploughed after the flood (or before if flow rate is negligible), damage is likely to be much less, provided slopes are gentle, e.g. at Dafort.

II THE EFFECTS OF HUMAN ACTIVITY ON THE ENVIRONMENT AND THE EVOLUTION OF THE VILLAGE LAND SYSTEMS

Throughout the preceding paragraphs we found ourselves stressing repeatedly that the most important changes undergone recently by the environment resulted less from natural factors than from human intervention. The latter can be divided into two large categories: reactions to the drought, and the evolution of the spatial organisation of the utilised lands as a response to the phenomenon of migration. We shall examine each of these categories in succession.

1. *The reaction of human groups to the drought*

The activities which have had the most important consequences at a regional level are without doubt those of the nomadic herders. Although there has been a significant loss of domestic grazing animals during the drought (estimates vary upwards from 50 per cent), enforced southward movement of nomadic herds has resulted in local devastation of the environment. Traditional migratory zones are to the east of the Assaba massif, and further west of the Garfa system. A relatively minor routeway, down the west of the Assaba massif, would seem to have become more important during the drought years. A traditional dry-season migration down these routeways to the river lands of the Senegal became more difficult during the dry period. Because of the lack of rains, and consequent poor forage, it seems that nomads were forced to fell large swaths of trees alongside the migratory pathways. Evidence of wholesale felling, particularly of *Acacia senegal* and *Acacia seyal*, whose forage value is good, at least for goats, was found north of Selibabi along the route to Hassi Chaggar, Mbedia, Dafort, Ndieo. The present landscape in these areas presents a very parched appearance with few surviving trees left standing. Those few that escaped the cutting are usually such thorny and unpalatable species as *Balanites aegyptiaca, Zizyphus mauritiana* and *Guiera senegalensis*. These concentrated zones of clearance stand in contrast to the more extensive areas of surviving savanna away from the routes. Restriction of cattle movement to these pathways has resulted in poor forage up to the present, at the same time as good pasture exists in the areas between tracks. Lack of utilisation of these superior pastures is due to inadequate water supply. The zone of animal movement southwards through Ndieo, Dafort etc. is based upon the fact that the villages, which are primarily agricultural, are located close to the better-quality lands of the valley bottom (especially the Garfa and its tributaries). It is in these locations that water supply is most reliable, hence the concentration of cattle movement. For the better pastures to be utilised, new wells would have to be dug, the animal movements taking place in the dry season when surface water has disappeared. The advisability of constructing new water supplies in order to shift grazing pressure away from the present zones of degradation is questionable. Similar attempts to disperse grazing through selected establishment of new water supplies elsewhere in West Africa have resulted in lateral spread of overgrazing. Instead of releasing pressure, dispersion has merely transferred it. Nevertheless, good pasture exists in Mauritania, and long-term improvement of livestock must eventually involve its utilisation.

The ultimate dry-season goal of the nomads are the river areas close to the Senegal itself. In the uncultivated areas of the *walo, fonde* and *djedjogol*, surface water supplies are adequate until the ensuing rains enable the herds to return to the north. Animals are concentrated on both the Mauritanian and the Senegalese sides of the river, and also along the Karakoro. The same type of tree felling witnessed in the north is also observable close to the river. It is compounded by the activities of local farmers and village dwellers. Trees are cut for domestic fuel and construction purposes, and for the preparation of new farmlands (see below for a fuller discussion of this aspect of clearance). Within the river lands wholesale destruction of trees was observed north of Gouraye, south of Moulessimou, and west of Mouderi.

Dramatic changes in vegetation and ground cover have not been the responsibility solely of the nomads. One outcome of the difficulties of stock rearing during the drought was the purchase of animals by the sedentary, farming Soninke.[5] Cattle, sheep and goats acquired at this time have been grazed close to the villages, and in many cases brought inside the compounds for protection during the night. Daily movement to and from, and around, villages has resulted in overgrazing and devastation in addition to that caused by the nomads. This is particularly evident in the northern Soninke areas of Mauritania. Many villages are surrounded by a zone (sometimes 2 km. radius) where vegetation of any form has completely disappeared. The quantities of manure which cover these areas are little used at present, and bare soil is exposed to erosion when the rains begin.

In summary, the need to maintain both food and water supplies for domestic herbivores has resulted in extreme, though concentrated pressure on the vegetation, leading to complete clearance, and subsequent soil exposure in some areas. It is not possible to be precise about the possibility of recovery, but experiments in other areas of Mauritania,[6] Chad,[7] and the Sudan[8] indicate that with freedom from grazing, re-establishment of both grass and tree cover is likely, though the time-scale is unpredictable.

The second phenomenon which must be considered, but only partially, as a response of the farmers to the new climatic conditions of these last years, is certain changes in the location of farming activities within the land systems. This general tendency is observable throughout the Guidimaka as well as in Senegal. It is characterised by a tendency to abandon the high lands (*dieri*) in favour of intermediary zones, which up till then were less cultivated, such as the lower *fonde* in the riverine areas, and the slopes of the depressions (*paraole*) in the villages of the interior. These changes may be explained as an adaptation to lower rainfall, by the fact that sandy soils (*signa*) or sandy-silty soils (*katamagne*) have a lower water-retention capacity than the *fonde* or *paraole*. We have noted above the consequences of clearance of vegetation from the point of view of erosion, in the areas bordering Oued Garfa: the increase of sheetwash, gullying, or on the contrary the blocking of the channels and meandering. With regard to the alluvial lands of Senegal, the lowest areas of the *fonde*, difficult to cultivate in years of normal flood, have now been brought into cultivation as *dieri* lands have been abandoned. This is particularly

evident between Bakel and Mouderi, where the comparison
between 1960 air photographs and our own field observations in
1975 show quite clearly that a long strip of thick *fonde* vegetation
has been cleared. The *fonde noir* is not the only terrain that has
been recently cleared. At Mouderi, new *walo* lands have been
cleared of their natural *acacia nilotica* woodland and further
extension seems likely. This is particularly evident in the
north-western half of the large basin north-west of the village. It is
difficult for the time being to say whether this results from an
important demographic increase, or whether it is the consequence
of restrictions on cultivation by Senegalese citizens of lands within
Mauritanian territory, thus making it necessary for them to fall
back on the part of their village lands on the Senegalese side. The
desire to respond to the conditions created by the low floods, by
cultivating the lower areas, difficult to cultivate in normal years,
certainly must also be taken into account.

2. *The role of migration in the present evolution of the village land systems*

We have seen that the climatic conditions of these last few years
have brought about a certain number of changes in the way in
which human groups, mainly the farmers, exploit their environment. These modifications in a response to particular circumstances should not be allowed to obscure the fact that a more
fundamental and doubtless longer-lasting evolution is affecting the
whole of the land systems of the Guidimaka, from the point of view
of their functioning as well as of their structure.

(a) *The narrowing of the range of crops grown in the different zones of the agricultural land.*

Some noteworthy changes have occurred in the crops grown on
certain categories of land, most particularly on the *dieri*. On the
higher ground there has been an extremely noticeable cut-back in
groundnut cultivation, which is becoming more and more marginal
within the total of agricultural production. With millet it has been
mainly the long-cycle varieties (*sagno*) which have been affected.

One can certainly ascribe climatic causes to these phenomena,
the drought of recent years having discouraged the cultivation of
those crops which need most water. This is certainly true of the
long-cycle millet. None the less it seems that, in the case of
groundnuts, the general decline is without doubt linked to the
growth of migration. Because of the drain on the labour force, the
women, who in Soninke culture have the monopoly of groundnut

cultivation, have had to redirect their efforts towards the production of cereals, especially sorghum. In this connection, the growth in purchasing power resulting from migrants' remittances, and the growth of consumption of a substitute product in the form of industrial groundnut oil, have certainly helped this transfer.

This decline should be seen in connection with the progressive disappearance of cotton and indigo, formerly grown by the women of the *fonde*. Thus, we can see an overall picture of impoverishment of the range of crops grown, corresponding to an increased dependence of the village economy on external supplies, and a retreat in the production system to basic foodstuffs.

(b) *The contraction of the agricultural land*
In fact, the phenomenon which we have just described forms part of a much wider tendency: the gradual abandonment of the higher land, in favour of the *fonde* fields in the riverside areas, and in favour of the slopes of the depressions (*paraole*) in the villages of the interior.

Certainly, climatic factors played an undoubted role in this evolution. However, they are not by themselves a sufficient explanation. For example, where the *dieri* is close to the village (e.g. Diaguili and Harr), the tendency to withdrawal is less marked. Conversely, in Gabou in Senegal, the total abandonment of a zone of *signa*, situated at the foot of a cuesta of the Continental Terminal, is undoubtedly due to its distance from the village; a difficulty compounded by a lack of water points, necessitating frequent journeys to and fro and thereby demanding an excessive amount of time and effort.

The decrease in the available labour force as a consequence of migration has, without doubt, played an important role in setting off these movements to abandon the higher land. In our analysis of the agricultural calendar, we stressed the strong competition existing between the cultivation of the *fonde* (or of the *paraole*) and that of the *dieri*. In a situation where the available work-force is insufficient and when the distance of the *dieri* imposes a substantial loss of time and effort, it is clear that such a contradiction cannot but be resolved at the expense of the *dieri*. What we find is a contraction of the cultivated land towards the areas closest to its agricultural centre; the areas near the river in the case of the riverside villages and the depressions in the case of the villages of the interior.

(c) *Stagnation in areas cultivated*
These various comments bring us to the problem of the changes in

the extent of areas cultivated. It is sometimes said that a consequence of the migratory phenomenon has been a very marked reduction in cultivated area. In absolute terms this tendency is not clear. Abandonment of some areas of land is in fact probably compensated for by clearing in other zones of the village land.

We must take account, none the less, of the specific situation of each village. For example, at Harr and Oulombome, where the problem of replacement of the labour of absent migrants seems quite pressing, we were told that a significant number of families can now no longer cultivate such large areas as they used to cultivate some decades ago.

A detailed and systematic study would be necessary to give a precise answer to this question. One thing that is certain, however, is that if there has been no reduction there has at least been stagnation in the area cultivated within the Guidimaka area as a whole. In 1923 it was estimated that the total area cultivated with the Cercle of the Guidimaka lay in the region of 17,500 ha (Saint Pere, 1925). In 1972, official estimates for the agricultural 'secteur' of Selibabi were of 16,800 ha. Of course the boundaries of the former Cercle and of the 'secteur agricole' do not exactly coincide. It seems, moreover, that the more recent estimate is a considerable underestimate. The comparison is none the less still enlightening, as it would not have been possible, in any case, to arrive at totals so close to one another if the Guidimaka had seen in these last fifty years massive clearances and cultivation of vast areas of new land — as has happened in the greater part of the Sudano-Sahelian Africa.

The stagnation of areas cultivated is therefore certain. Given even a slight demographic increase, this represents without doubt a substantial reduction in cultivated area per inhabitant.

Here again, it is the phenomenon of migration which provides the basis for an explanation. First of all, the drain on the labour force has played an important role, but it has probably been limited in effect through the employment of seasonal workers who are recruited locally (Peuls and Moors, previously non-farmers) or from Mali. At a deeper level of analysis, it is doubtless the marginal position of the agricultural production system within an economy oriented towards the exterior and dominated by migration (the only activity from which a monetary surplus may be expected). This explains the lethargy manifest in the stagnation of cultivated areas. In the present situation, the only function of agriculture is to provide the necessary minimum subsistence for those who remain in the villages: the mainspring of social and economic activity is turned towards the exterior.

To conclude these reflections on the environmental dynamics and the contemporary evolution of the cultivated lands in the Mauritanian Guidimaka, as well as in the nearby regions of Senegal, we can say without doubt that there have been major changes within the last decade, in the natural environment as well as in the forms of land-use practised by local people.

This evolution is perhaps less apparent in the alluvial lands in Senegal, where casual observation would suggest that they are still well-wooded. However, a more careful observation (at Lobali, for example — a small village downstream) indicates that the natural vegetation cover there is far more dense and widespread than in the main cultivation areas further south.

The woodlands that still exist in the latter zone, both the *walo* and the *fonde* communities, are degraded and below the natural potention of the environment. Where uncleared, the partial cutting by nomads, and the extent of secondary bush (as shown by the prevalence of *Balanites aegyptiaca, Guiera senegalensis, Zizyphus spp.* and *Calotripis procera*), indicate a broad-scale and progressive deterioration of the natural vegetation.

In these low-lying areas, as in the *dieri*, the main factors for change have been the reactions of human groups to the drought and the evolution of the spatial organisation of the cultivated land as a result of new conditions created by migration.

Smaller factors of change have come into operation here and there. We shall emphasise two of them in particular:

Fires. In the dry savannah, fire is a natural phenomenon, whose incidence increases with population density. Its effects tend to be those of a general deterioration, although short-term benefits may accrue (initiation of new grass growth, local and temporary enrichment of the soil). In comparison to Nigeria and Niger, burning does not appear to be a major problem on the Senegalese side of the river. However, officials in Selibabi expressed considerable concern with respect to the situation in Mauritania. At present it seems to be a problem of less than major proportions, although the long-term outlook, without controls, is less encouraging.

Wood-collecting for the provision of domestic fuel and construction materials. The immediate surroundings of Bakel, Gouraye, Dafort, Selibabi and Bouanze are now virtually devoid of trees. There is no doubt that considerable time and effort is now put into the transportation of domestic wood fuel into Bakel, and this situation can only be intensified in the future as population continues to increase. The ultimate extreme of this situation is witnessed in Kano, Nigeria, where an important commerce is involved in the import of firewood from a radius of up to 20 km., with the same transport carrying manure away in the evening (Mortimore and Wilson, 1965). Although fuel shortage of this magnitude is unlikely to become important at Bakel, the social and economic effects of the development of trade in this commodity may well have repercussions in other spheres.

However definite the localised signs of degradation of vegetation and soils may be, it is none the less true that the general situation in the Guidimaka with regard to environmental potential remains largely favourable. This is a very important point for the prospects for agricultural development in the region. This is a great contrast to so many other lands of Sudano-Sahelian Africa, where the over-exploited physical environment only just manages to support the functioning of agricultural systems which have been extended to their extreme limits.

From the point of view of availability of land, the overall situation is positive. Indeed, the stagnation of agriculture over recent years left free large areas of good-quality soil. Certainly, technical improvements and a good deal of care will be necessary to exploit them, but the possibilities for development are none the less real.

Such an optimistic overall diagnosis should not be allowed to obscure the existence of sub-zones where, by contrast, the situation remains fairly worrying, due to an apparent lack of cultivable land. The settlement of former nomads, particularly in the Ndieo region, the destruction of vegetation, and the changing pattern of land-use resulting from the drought, have all led to a perceived shortage of land resources. From the viewpoint of the physical environment, there appear to be alternatives to the existing field systems of the alluvial lands. At Ndieo, for example, the soils bordering the major oued west of the village are in fact considerably more fertile than those at present used for rice cultivation. Water supply could be a problem, but simple techniques such as complete tillage of the soil, surface mulching, or the construction of water-retaining banks might improve the water-retention capacity of the soils. If existing farmlands can be improved, higher yields might offset the need for extra land. The use of locally produced manure which is available in large quantities can help in this situation.

The preference for alluvial areas which are inundated each year creates the shortage of land. Alternative *dieri* lands are available at Ndieo and possibly Dafort and Bouanze and, providing farming techniques can be adapted to these new areas, it seems more sensible to cultivate these rather than create new alluvial lands by the construction of dams. It is clear, however, that this question is part of the wider problem of the overall relations between human groups and their environment. Multiple non-technical factors, including social, cultural and economic factors, are definitely involved, and any practical proposals for change must necessarily take them into account. What is certain, and what we have stressed, is that one cannot say that there is, even in the least favourable cases, a real lack of land; that is to say the exhaustive utilisation of existing environmental potential.

From the point of view of the evolution of vegetation, and of erosion, the inherent stability of the various sytems of the region is open to discussion. Their relative susceptibilities to disturbance, and capacities for recovery, can only be tentatively assumed at this stage. The *walo* areas are continually losing their vegetation and, though capable of rapid recovery, continual disturbance is unlikely to permit this. However, the annual flood, and the inherent qualities of the soils, suggest that long-term productivity can be maintained. *Fonde* areas also have the capacity for rapid re-colonisation by vegetation, though soil fertility will always tend to be low because of low clay content. Here, too, grazing and cutting are likely to arrest any real development. The *dieri*, because of its seasonality, is more fragile. The generally poorer soils, low water status, and naturally sparser vegetation make the effects of burning, clear felling and overgrazing more permanent. In the long term, increasing population density both of animals and people may produce semi-permanent degradation. Soil erosion may follow such disturbance, and once this has occurred the establishment of a new equilibrium is much more difficult and possibly unattainable. With the exception of a few particular areas, a process of this type is not yet at work at the level of the region. On the contrary, the available areas of *dieri* constitute an important reserve of land which could, if used with caution, become a very advantageous factor in the agricultural development of the region.

Finally, let us note that, of all the areas visited, the interior alluvial lands of the Guidimaka seem, as we have stressed before, the most fragile under present patterns of use. Erosion, now confined to small areas, may well increase in magnitude and extent without well-formulated management schemes. Out of all of the Guidimaka region, it is clear that this area requires the most urgent action. However, before this can be undertaken and new techniques introduced, more intensive studies will be necessary.

NOTES

1 It has been thought that the viability of the seeds of the annual grasses which form an important component of the Sahelian prairies (particularly in the north) declines after only one or two years. Consequently, with a drought of five or six years' duration, insufficient viable seed would be left to recolonise the drought lands when adequate rains finally commence.

2 We did not see the more extensive dunes to the east of the Assaba massif.

3 Remedial action may take the form of a surface mulch or repeated tillage of the soil to break up the crust.

4 A channel with excess energy (through increased run-off) can erode downwards and headwards if slopes are steep, erode laterally if slopes are shallow, or expend surplus energy in increasing sediment load. In the case of Ndiéo, the first action seems likely. In the case of Dafort and Bouanze, the latter two are more probable.

5 Largely encouraged by the very low prices at which the nomads, hard-pressed by the famine, were forced to sell their animals.

6 Adam (1968).

7 Depierre et Gillet (1971).

8 Halwagy (1962).

CHAPTER 10

Agricultural and Pastoral Techniques: Levels of Consumption and Production

In the preceding section we analysed the agricultural production systems from the point of view of their overall functioning, and of their internal coherence or disequilibrium. It is useful now to go into greater detail and give a general description of the techniques practised; and to try, with a great deal of caution, to evaluate their immediate efficiency (that is to say, how they contribute to both the level of crop yield and the satisfaction of basic food needs). We must again stress that, given the conditions under which this study was carried out (in particular the brevity of the field study), we are not in a position to give reliable statistical estimates at this stage. It is only on the basis of the determination of the order of magnitude and a qualitative grasp of the mechanisms which are too significant to be missed, that we can claim to establish our diagnosis.

I AGRICULTURAL TECHNIQUES

1. *Dryland farming*

In the Guidimaka, dry-land cultivation involves two main land systems, the *fonde* and the *dieri*. Given the limited surface area that it represents, and the clearly defined system of allocating access that operates there, the *fonde* is used constantly and regularly. Certainly, extensive areas are sometimes left fallow for periods of up to seven years, or even more, especially where the land is far from the village. None the less, the division of the land into plots which are the lasting property of certain family groups ensures a relative continuity in their agricultural use.

In the *dieri*, on the other hand, the situation is completely different. In effect, despite the fact that the higher lands, as with the general order of village land, come under the authority of the family group with hereditary rights to the chieftainship, no one family group may abrogate to itself specific user rights over any particular portion of uncultivated land. In principle, then, the *dieri* is open to all and in fact, given the amount of space available, we see a great mobility of the plots which are cultivated on it. The farmers are continually prospecting: in the middle of the vast stretches of bush available, they are searching for zones which they think will be the most favourable to them, given the climatic conditions and the crops which they wish to grow. The decisive factor in the abandonment of plots previously cultivated is the lowering of soil fertility, which is made manifest in the progressive decline of yields and the appearance of parasitic plants such as *Striga*. There seems to be a double rhythm governing the alternation of periods of cultivation and fallow:

(i) Long fallow periods: Vast areas, containing a large number of fields, are cleared from the bush and kept under cultivation over several tens of years, and are then left, while new areas which have never been cultivated or have been long abandoned are in their turn cleared and put down to crops.

(ii) Short fallow cycles: Within these vast areas which are exploited for long periods, the fields are alternately cultivated and left fallow according to a shorter cycle. The succession of crops and of fallow periods does not follow a rigid model. In practice, it depends particularly on the nuances of quality of the soil. Thus the *signa*, or sandy soil, is exhausted much more quickly than heavier soil, and it may be left fallow after two years of cropping and for five or six years. Another factor is the succession of crops that have been grown; that is to say, whether one crop has been continuously cultivated or, on the contrary, cereals and legumes have been alternated.

Generally speaking, as far as the *dieri* is concerned, there is no systematic rotation of crops within a fixed area, but rather a great mobility of crops within the available village lands. This is a sign of the continuing quest for adaptation to the changing conditions of the environment. This is an important fact, for it indicates one of the directions in which an improvement in traditional techniques must be sought, if a greater mastery of the environment is to be achieved.

Once they have chosen the plot to be cultivated in the next rainy season, the farmers go on to the first agricultural task, strictly speaking that of land clearing.

(a) *Land Clearing*

This task is usually undertaken by the men because it is physically demanding. It takes place during the period just before the rains in May or June. Two typical situations may be observed:

(i) On the *fonde* or *dieri* which have already been cultivated the previous year, little work is required. Most often maize stalks and various other debris have been left on the soil, which has the double advantage of ensuring effective protection against erosion, and bringing a significant amount of organic matter into the soil.

(ii) On new plots being prepared from virgin land, much more work is required. It is necessary to cut the tops off the trees, fell the big bushes, and clear the ground of underbrush. In these cases fire is generally used, which is rarely the case in the first situation. A study of the labour-time employed would be necessary to establish precisely the work-load of clearing new plots. Although we have no evidence on this point, we may assume, in any case, that the lack of labour resulting from emigration could constitute a real obstacle to the mobility of plots.

(b) *Preparation of the soil*

The preparation of the soil prior to sowing is an agricultural practice that is known to and applied by the Guidimaka farmers. Since it is done by hand and with rudimentary tools, it cannot be extended beyond limited areas. Small fields are thus the object of particular attention. This is most particularly the case with the cattle enclosures which are near the villages and which are used for growing maize. Some time after the first rains, when the soil has begun to lose its hardness, it is turned over with a hoe (Plate XVI), just deeply enough to bury the manure and vegetable matter, in particular the new-grown grass.

Although spatially limited, the existence of this practice is a positive point in that it shows that local farmers already have relatively elaborate traditional techniques, the use of which eventually may be usefully extended. In this case, one of the limiting factors will most certainly be the lack of available labour force, and therefore the need to bring in new technical tools may well emerge within a short time.

(c) *Sowing*

Sowing usually begins as soon as the first usable rains (20-40 mm.) appear. If the ground has been prepared, the seeds are simply placed on the ridges, but the holes in the ground are deep enough for the plants' roots to develop in the firm soil beneath. If the ground has not been prepared, holes of 10-20 cm. depth are made at each footstep with a small hoe (*sakade*) (Plate XIV) held in the right hand. The seeds (5 or 10 per hole for sorghum) are scattered from a small calabash held in the left hand (Plate XV). Very often this calabash will contain seeds of different varieties and even species, for example, different types of sorghum and some seeds of cowpeas. Distribution occurs, therefore, according to chance by what comes to the sower's hand. This practice could be aimed at combating the climatic risks — varieties of differing lengths of cycle being mixed. It could also have other ends, the effectiveness of which are difficult to assess: for example, to keep off birds or monkeys by introducing some varieties which are considered repulsive to them.

It should also be noted that dry sowing is quite frequently practised, particularly when the rains are late.

Fungal treatment of the seeds is very rare, as are practices designed to encourage greater root development. Furthermore, they do not generally apply either manure or fertiliser, except in the plots near the village where maize is grown, in which case animal manure is used. It is worth noting that this practice could bring about an appreciable improvement in fertility, if it were practised regularly. This could also be the point of departure for the consideration of the use of other techniques, such as the use of 'green manure' and the introduction of vegetable matter into the soil.

In theory, all the family take part in this operation of sowing. If it has not rained within ten days of sowing, it is often necessary to repeat this task several times.

(d) *Crop husbandry*

A week or fifteen days after the plants appear, hoeing begins. At least two hoeings are necessary, and in the case of millet the ground has to be completely cleaned.

For all cereals, and at the same time as hoeing, thinning-out to two or three shoots per hole is necessary. The seedlings which are dug out are replanted in those places where seeds have not germinated. The number of shoots left in each hole seems to have a large influence on the final yield. Tests must be carried out to study this technique more closely, and to evaluate its effects as a function of the different types of soils. It should be noted that this work is generally done by the men, and very rarely by the women.

From flowering time to harvest, the guarding of the cultivated fields is essential because of the attacks of different animals, in particular birds. When the fields are near to a village, this work is often done by the children. On the other hand, when the fields are a long way away, this work is the responsibility of the men. In such cases, it often happens that some members of the family temporarily move out of the village to a settlement near the fields which is especially built for the purpose. Where plots are contiguous, a collective organisation is sometimes established so that each of the neighbours takes his turn at guard duty. In estimated worker-hours, this is a very heavy task which enormously reduces the labour force available for other activities. This can lead to competition between tasks, for example in the riverside area where, in years when the flood is high, the work of guarding coincides in time with the clearing and sowing of the *walo*.

(e) *The Harvest*
Harvesting begins when the grain is ripe, sometimes before if the presence of birds jeopardises the whole crop. In the case of cereals, the task consists of cutting off the ears with either knives or sickles, or by hand, as is the case with maize. The ears are then tied into sheaves and left on the spot to dry for a period which may extend from a week to a month. Finally, when dried they are threshed, or stored as they are.

The selection of seeds for next year's sowing occurs prior to harvesting, which allows not only the choice of the most productive plants but also the retention for other characteristics, such as height, which makes harvesting easier.

(f) *Health factors*
Diseases and insect attacks are frequent in the rainy season, but at present it is not possible to estimate their precise effect on yield. In recent years, after the period of drought, there have been some attacks by locusts, with disastrous results on harvests.

2. *Flood-retreat Agriculture*

The second major type of cultivation starts as the flood waters recede. Contrary to practice on the *dieri* or the *fonde*, there is little choice as to the positioning of the fields. Most of them are cultivated each year, without fallow periods. The area to be sown is essentially determined by the height of the flood and the availability of labour.

(a) *Land clearing*
The preparation of the *walo* for cultivation is a long and difficult job. It often demands several years of work, since in the majority of cases the land supports dense stands of *Acacia nilotica*. Once initial clearance is finished, there still remains the annual removal of fresh growth following flood retreat. This task constitutes a bottleneck in years of high flood, because it coincides with the

harvesting or guarding of the maize and short-cycle sorghum on the *dieri* and *fonde*, and these tasks cannot be delayed or neglected without great losses in yield. On this question, some experiments, where land is cleared before flooding begins, have been tried in the Kaedi region. At this time the competition for labour is much less. As a result of this earlier scheduling of the work, the soil remains clean after the flood and is ready to be sown rapidly, which makes possible the extension of the growth period and ultimately an increase in yield. In any case, this technique could be tried out, so long as the special characteristics of each village are taken into account.

(b) *Sowing*

Three weeks after the retreat of the flood water, sowing begins. Its timing has a great effect upon the yields. This task is probably the only one where some specialisation or differentiation of work within the family is shown. It is organised as a sequence of activities: the man comes first, and with two or three strokes of the hoe digs in the surface crust a hole 6-8 cm. deep. After him, the woman, armed with a pointed stick 5-8 cm. in diameter, makes a hole in the same place, 20 cm. deep, and in this a child places the seeds, adds a handful of sand, and finally fills the hole. The distance between the holes is approximately one metre. No manure or fertiliser is added and no treatment is given to the seed.

(c) *Crop Husbandry*

The most important job is hoeing, which begins 15-20 days after the appearance of the plant. The basic aim is to remove the weeds and to keep the soil open. This work may be repeated two or three times. Between the first and second hoeing, there is the thinning-out. Two or three plants are left in each hole, and the replanting of the plants that have been thinned permits the replacement of those that have failed. According to trials at Kaedi, there may be a close relationship between the number of plants left in each hole, and the level of yields. Weeding is slow work, and it is estimated that a good worker could complete 400 square metres per day. Viewed another way, weeding takes 25 days per hectare. Because of its arduous nature, this work is reserved for the men.

From flowering to harvest-time guarding is necessary. In the case of flood-retreat agriculture, this not only affords protection from birds and wild animals, such as monkeys and wart-hogs, but also from cattle straying from transhumant herds which arrive at the riverside at this time of year.

(d) *Harvest*

This work is similar to that carried out for the dry-land crops. However, the period required to dry the ears is much shorter and takes about a week.

II LEVELS OF AGRICULTURAL PRODUCTION AND THE PROBLEM OF CLIMATIC RISK

1. *A tentative evaluation of production levels*

In the absence of systematic measurements taken by ourselves, we have to rely on the assessments of official sources, or of studies that have preceded ours. As always in such cases, these figures must be viewed with a good deal of caution.

(a) *Relative surface-areas*

According to the reports of the Selibabi Secteur Agricole, the proportion of each crop produced in relation to total surfaces cultivated in a normal year is as follows:

70% sorghum (45% *fella*, 55% *nienico*)
10% maize
 8% millet
 6% groundnuts
 4% rice

Cowpea cultivation is included in the total for cereals, and there is no separate estimate of the true area that it occupies.

(b) *Yields*

Yields are difficult to determine because of the great number of varieties cultivated and of their variable response to different soils. However, according to the Secteur Agricole, we can consider the following figures as an average estimate.

Crop	Yield		
fella sorghum	700-800 kg. per ha		
nienico sorghum	400-600 ''	''	''
millet	450-650 ''	''	''
groundnuts	400-650 ''	''	''
maize	650-850 ''	''	''

Some approximate estimates which we ourselves have made in the field (by reconstituting local estimates of the previous harvest) have given higher figures, particularly for a rainy-season sorghum (*nabane*) which is grown on the *fonde*. In this case we have estimated that the yield must be around 1,500 kg. per ha. Although this figure could not in itself form a very reliable basis for calculations, none the less it does lead us to suppose that the figures above are slightly underestimated. If this were confirmed, it would show that in terms of yield per unit area, the success of the traditional technical system is far from negligible. This would agree very well with the observations we have made concerning the low intensity of exploitation of the natural environment.

(c) *The area of cultivated land*
The total area of cultivated land in the Département of Selibabi in 1972 was estimated at 16,800 ha. Even more than the other figures, this should be considered with caution. The local technical services have available far from the necessary means to carry out such an evaluation, even with the minimum of accuracy. It is clear, however, that any development activity undertaken in the Département must, as a first step, assemble basic data on the total area cultivated, production levels, and yields.

Using for the moment the official figures, we arrive at the following estimates of annual production achieved for the different crops per year:

Crop	Production
sorghum	6284 tonnes
millet	756 ”
groundnuts	537 ”
maize	873 ”

With a population figure of 45,000, this would then correspond to a per capita cereal consumption of less than 200 kilos per annum. A deficit is suggested, but this remains to be verified through a more detailed analysis in the future.

(d) *Labour productivity*
Studies carried out in recent years by the B.D.P.A. and the S.E.D.E.S. on the one hand, and by the S.O.G.R.E.A.H.[1] on the other, give the following estimates:

Areas cultivated per person: *dieri* 0.27 ha, *walo* 0.17 ha.
Hours of work (without crop-guarding): *dieri* — 70 days per ha, *walo* — 80 days per ha.

It should be noted that these estimates are quite close to those given by other sources for Toucouleur farming in the Senegal river valley.
These are the only quantitative estimates that are possible at the

current stage of our research. In our analysis of the agricultural system such generalisations are of little or no value, and for us it is better to rely on a cautious and reasonable 'qualitative' approach rather than on statistical evaluations with a false appearance of accuracy.

2. The problems of climatic risk

It is certain that, whatever the degree of accuracy attained, any evaluation of the level of efficiency of the agrarian system based on average yields would not take into account the actual conditions under which agricultural production takes place. In this context there is one very important point to be taken into consideration, that of the variations in climatic conditions and the resultant risk for agricultural production.

World opinion has been made very much aware of this by the succession of dry years which has just occurred. Certainly, this has been an exceptional event, both in its length and its severity. None the less, it would be misleading to seek an explanation of the current difficulties of agriculture in the Guidimaka by sole reference to this 'accident'. Indeed, although departures from the 'mean' are not usually so large, variability in climatic elements is a constant factor in the Sahelian situation. This is clearly shown in the probability estimates contained in Table I and Appendix B(i), where low annual rainfall is shown to be quite frequent.

Where rainfall is concerned, reference to annual totals offers a first approach. Not only are there important variations in time from one year to another, but also in space, as rainfall measurements taken at two points quite close to each other, Bakel River and Bakel Airfield, show that each year over the period 1955-65 there was a mean difference of the order of 25 per cent (see Appendix B(ii)). However, in fact the annual total is only a secondary aspect of the relationship between rainfall and agricultural production. A year with a high rainfall total may produce a bad harvest, and vice versa. The two most important aspects from the point of view of agricultural yields are, firstly, the date of the first serviceable rain, which has very important repercussions in particular on the choice of the variety to be sown and on the choice of zone to be cultivated, and, secondly, the distribution of rain throughout the rainy season and how well it corresponds to the needs of the plants. Thus, millet needs rain within ten days of sowing, and then regular rainfall during the vegetative growth, but has much smaller needs as soon as flowering occurs, when heavy rains could be damaging.

Where the flood pattern is concerned, the most important elements are the height of the flood, which influences the extent of the cultivable areas, and the date when the waters recede, a late retreat having noticeable ill-effects on yields.

In both rainfall and flood patterns the data given in Part I, Chapter 2, and the accompanying Tables and Appendices, show the intensity of annual variations; this gives an idea of the conditions of great insecurity within which the peasants work.

This notion of riskiness should be borne in mind when making any attempt to intervene in the agricultural production system. To answer the real anxieties of the farmers, any projects undertaken must have as their first objective the diminution of their vulnerability in the face of climatic variations.

III ANIMAL HUSBANDRY

In the Selibabi region there is a substantial number of livestock, which is now in a recuperation phase after the losses of the drought years. (Losses are estimated at about 50 per cent by the local Service d'Elevage.) Current estimates are as follows for the Département:

cattle 64,000 head   sheep 17,000 head
goats 93,000 head   horses and donkeys 5,700 head

Most of the cattle are transhumant. The Soninke and Toucouleur cattle which remain near the villages represent altogether about 40 per cent of the total.

The transhumant movement of cattle begins at the end of December, and takes a north-south direction. The route is determined not only by the search for good pasture but also by the possibilities of finding water. These factors have led to the existence of two routes. Following the first, the cattle from the north (Kiffa) come southwards down the Karakoro river. Following the second, herds from the region near to Ajar-Sarakole move southwards towards the river, crossing the Oued Niorde between the villages of Testai and Harr. In both cases the return journey is by the same route. Generally, all along both routes are zones rich in good quality pasture, but in small quantities. Figure 11 illustrates these two major routeways, and a third, minor one, whose importance would seem to have grown during and since the 1968-73 drought.

The Peul and Maure are first-class cattlemen. They often take charge of the Soninke cattle, in exchange for remuneration either in cash or kind which, for a family herd of 15 cattle, corresponds to

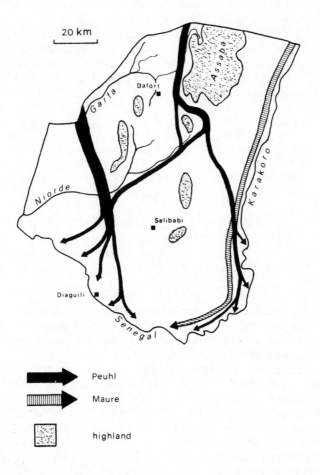

Fig. 11 Simplified cattle migration routes of Guidimaka

700-800 Ouguiyas[2] per year. This specialisation between herders and farmers is the basis of continuing exchanges between the two categories of producer: the former providing meat and milk, the latter millet, maize and various other agricultural products. None the less, at the level of sedentary agriculture there is negligible effective integration of livestock and agricultural activity.

Table X
The evolution of livestock prices in the Guidimaka (1971-74)

Livestock category	Price 1971 per animal (in Ouguiyas)	Price 1974 per animal (in Ouguiyas)
Young bull (12-18 mths, 130 kg.)	910	1 755
Young bull (24-30 mths, 180 kg.)	1 260	3 300
Young bull (36-40 mths, 220 kg.)	1 760	3 740
Mature bull (320 kg.)	2 720	5 600
Quality bull (400 kg.)	4 000	7 800
Culled cow (230 kg.)	1 380	3 910
Producing cow	2 600	5 600
Ewe or culled billy-goat (30 kg.)	300	465
Kid (approx. 12 kg.)	114	140

Stock management is extensive and production levels are lower than that expected from the local breeds, especially where Maure and Peul zebus are concerned. In both cases maturity is reached late (at about six years) and is rarely more than 350-450 kg., with a yield of 50 per cent. This situation is a serious limitation to the possible use of animal traction, since in good average conditions the total weight of a pair of oxen would be only about 550 kg. and these could only be used to work light soils. This fact should be constantly borne in mind whenever the introduction of animal traction is being considered.

Milk production yield is approximately 220-250 litres per year, with daily production going from 2 litres in the rainy season to half a litre in the dry season. These production levels are linked to multiple factors, such as the variable quality of forage, difficulties in finding water, the lack of mineral elements and the persistence of such diseases as trypanosomiasis and brucellosis in some areas.

Trading in the sale of animals on the hoof is mainly practised outside the region: in Senegal, Mali and to the Kaedi abattoir. Within the Guidimaka itself trading is relatively small, given the local consumption. Nevertheless, although it is impossible at the moment to estimate its extent, there does exist a very important tendency to transfer cattle from the specialised herders, Peul and Maure, to the Soninke farmers, who, as we have seen, invest a large part of their income from migration in cattle.

As for the types of animals sold, these vary according to the market. Culled cows are sold in Selibabi, while bullocks and heavier bulls are sold to middlemen who take them out of the area. These are shown in Table X.

The important differences to be observed between the two periods in the Table can be explained initially by the very low level of prices during the drought. This phenomenon was linked to the intensity of supply, which was itself the result not only of the necessity to sell which faced the local producers, but also of the saturation of their normal export markets, particularly in Senegal, because of the massive sales by farmers in the Southern areas.

In 1974, on the other hand, there was a strong increase which was the effect of a significant increase in demand, linked to the need to rebuild former stocks. This demand affected particularly the reproductive animals, which their owners are generally reluctant to part with. If favourable climatic conditions continue, the price of these reproductive animals may fall. On the other hand, where cattle for slaughter are concerned, prices could remain high throughout the period of reconstituting herds, especially if good results are achieved in the field of food production. The level of supply, in the case of cattle, is closely linked to the quantities and prices of the cereals that the herders must buy in order to ensure their subsistence.

In conclusion, we stress that in the Guidimaka, as in general throughout the Sahel, animal husbandry is a very important source of potential wealth. This is true not only for the specialised herders, the Peul and the Maure, but also in the case of the Soninke farmers. Indeed, the aptitude for herding which is shown by the latter is far from being equal to the enthusiasm they have shown in recent years for the accumulation of cattle. There is enormous progress to be made in this field, especially since the size of the herds available to most of the settled villages constitutes an important asset from the point of view of the development of agricultural production.

In so far as purely agricultural activities are concerned, we have had occasion several times to remark that important progress may be envisaged, particularly in the intensification of techniques. However, we must not forget that our knowledge of traditional practices and of the functional articulations which ensure their integration into a coherent agrarian system remains very superficial. No intervention should therefore be made before a substantial discussion with the peasants. Such a discussion should proceed to:

(i) reappraise, on the basis of the needs and knowledge of the peasants, the technical improvements whose efficiency may appear 'obvious' to the agronomist;

(ii) carry out simple experiments with those interested so as to perfect techniques which will effectively deal with the main factors causing bottlenecks in the agrarian system.

IV THE LEVEL OF CONSUMPTION

Here it is difficult to have precise data without detailed and systematic consumption surveys. However, on the basis of the different data that we have been able to collect through on-the-spot interviews, it is possible to formulate a general impression.

Generally, the information given by the Soninke and Toucouleur farmers brought out the existence of no large deficit in cereal produce. It seems, therefore, that in a normal year the present agricultural system is capable of ensuring a minimum consumption level which matches the generally acceptable[3] norm of 200 kg. of cereals per person per year. Furthermore, reserve supplies are often kept, and it is quite common for families to have in their granaries enough grain to feed them for several years. The recent period of drought, of course, has largely depleted these reserves.

In the field of food consumption, the distinction between the villages of the interior and those near the river again remains pertinent.

In the former, cereal consumption seems to be approximately 200 kg. per person per year. Rice accounts for a relatively modest part of this total: 15-20 kg. per person per year, of which a large part is produced locally.[4]

In the larger villages nearer the river, such as Diaguili, Diogountourou and Khabou, consumption seems to follow a different pattern. Cereals have a smaller overall importance at about 150 kg. per person per year, according to our enquiries. Furthermore, the place of rice in this total is much more important, increasing to 40 or 50 kg. per person per year. This difference is first of all due to the extra food provided by the natural environment in this zone, particularly from fishing and the *falo* crops (sweet potatoes). Thanks to these, the villagers are less dependent on cereals for their food. However, we should also see in this situation the effects of the migratory phenomenon, which is more marked and of much longer standing in these villages. Increased purchasing power and a certain modification of food habits are evident in the continuously increasing consumption, not only of rice, but also of cooking-oil (in some families, nearly a litre per day), sugar, bread,[5] tinned milk, coffee, biscuits, etc.

Even if the subsistence base continues to be ensured by local cereal production, it is clear that the Guidimaka's rural communities are becoming more and more dependent on the exterior, even at the level of food consumption. Thus the Selibabi Sonimex[6] sold more than 700 tons of imported rice in 1974 (the equivalent of the production of the whole region, according to official figures, which appear to be slightly over-estimated). If we take into account that to these official imports should be added all the rice which is smuggled in from Senegal, we see that the Selibabi region is actually dependent on the exterior for the greater part of its rice consumption. This situation may get substantially worse in the next few years, as the consumption of this cereal is continuing to grow.

The agricultural production system is tending more and more towards a marginal position in the local economy. Not only is it scarcely capable of generating the surplus which could lead to significant exchanges with the exterior,[7] but also, through the decline in its own production, it is ceding more and more to substitution foods imported from the outside.

As we noted in our discussion of the stagnation in the areas cultivated, we are dealing here with an agricultural system in a state of lethargy, one which is not even managing to reproduce the initial conditions necessary for its own functioning. Of course, agricultural production does remain an important element in the economic system as a whole, but it is still reduced to a supplementary role compared with the dominant place of emigration and the income which it supplies.

The result of this is a total absence of dynamism, which has made impossible any adaptive response to the large increase in purchasing power which has taken place over the last ten years. None the less, there does exist an important domestic market for those agricultural commodities such as rice, wheat, vegetables and fruit, which can be produced locally.

One of the principal objectives of any agricultural development project in this region must be to use this potential market as a springboard for growth in agricultural production.

NOTES

1. B.D.P.A.: Bureau pour le Développement de la Production Agricole.
S.E.D.E.S.: Société d'Etudes pour le Développement Economique et Social.
S.O.G.R.E.A.H.: Société Grenobloise d'Etudes et d'Aménagements Hydro-agricoles.
2. Between £7.80 and £8.90.
3. Particularly according to FAO criteria.
4. Some villages, such as Ndieo, are totally self-sufficient in rice.
5. In many villages, even in the interior, we find bakers who buy large quantities of wheat flour, producing bread in the village.
6. The regional office of the national Sonimex organisation, which has the monopoly of a certain number of current consumption products, such as rice, sugar and tea.
7. The problem of surpluses is, obviously, a very complex one. We note, and we shall come back to this, the continuation of the exchange of cereals within the region and towards the exterior, but in the absence of a detailed study of the true conditions under which commercial circulation takes place within the rural community, it is difficult to say whether these exchanges really involve surpluses, or whether they are the sign of accumulation taking place in the hands of one category of the population, at the expense of another.

CHAPTER 11

Outline of some Socio-economic Problems

In the context of the socio-economic field, we shall limit ourselves to supplementing the essentially technical observations which we have so far made with some general remarks on a certain number of fundamental points: the system of land tenure; organisation of production within the family; and the place of agriculture within the regional and national economy.

I THE SYSTEM OF LAND TENURE

Our analysis of the land-tenure system will be very brief. On the question of traditional collective norms, a number of studies have already been completed, both among the Toucouleur and among the Soninke (Boutillier and Cantrelle, op.cit.; Pollet and Winter, 1971). It would be very useful to develop from these a series of precise studies based on a detailed map of the village land plot by plot. It is the only way by which it would be possible to measure the difference between social 'theory' and actual practice. Obviously, this would be quite outside the limits of the field study that we have undertaken. We shall therefore restrict ourselves to a few remarks which to us seem to be of particular importance.

Traditionally, both Soninke and Toucouleur societies do not recognise individual property rights over land. The use of land is controlled by family groups: clans, extended families. On inheritance, the land left to a kinship group must remain undivided and continue to be worked collectively under the authority of the successor to the deceased family head. No one, whatever his status, in theory has the right to separate even a part of the family land by selling it. Although there have been some changes in this field, definitive selling of land in exchange for money is still very rare.

In a village with abundant *dieri*, access to such land is free. Any person who wishes to may clear as much bush land as he thinks he can work. When he abandons the worked land, anyone else may cultivate it in turn.[1]

The tenure system is completely different in the alluvial lands. These are subject to a form of distribution and control which is very rigid and fundamentally inegalitarian, representing a projection on to the soil of traditional social structures which are organised according to a rigidly hierarchical system. Soninke society, like the Toucouleur, is effectively divided into different castes: nobles, artisans and slaves. The latter two are generally excluded from any control over land. Among the nobles, it is generally the members of the founding family, that of the village chief, who control the major part of the village land.

Nevertheless, in the villages near the river, which were founded a long time ago, other noble clans may own a greater or lesser amount of land, given to them in former times as a gift.

Thus, a large proportion of the inhabitants of a village have, in relation to the soil which they work, only a user's right, granted by the 'master of the land' (*nyinyagumme*), the head of the family which controls land attribution. In many cases, the user's right may not be taken away from those who enjoy it; it may be passed on through inheritance. It is linked with an obligation to offer a payment in kind (*nyinyantiekhe*), of variable amount, which may be as little as a few 'mouds'[2] of grain (a payment of symbolic value), or as much as a tenth of the harvest. Even if this represents a sizeable contribution to the 'masters of the land', within the context of the existing local economy it cannot be considered as a significant form of accumulation. Compared with the monetary flows associated with emigration, the value of the produce circulating via these channels is certainly negligible.

Besides this mode of devolution of land rights, which is part of the traditional hierarchical relationship between individuals and family groups, there are other types of transfer of land which are more precarious and closer to purely commercial exchanges. This is so with certain forms of 'leasing' (*muso*), under which a landowner gives temporary cultivation rights over a plot for one agricultural season, in exchange for a third of the harvest, or for a half, if the landowner also provides the seed. At our present level of analysis, we can do no more than point to the existence of these types of contract, without being able to say whether they are marginal, or whether they affect a large number of farmers or large areas of land.

In any case, it does not seem that the land distribution system which exists in the Guidimaka gives rise, at the moment, to any important social tensions. Because of the stagnation of agricultural production, the scarcity of available labour and the low productivity of the technical means employed, there exist abundant reserves of most types of land. For the moment, therefore, competition is scarcely apparent in this area. On the other hand, given a structure which is so fundamentally inegalitarian, it is very difficult to say what might be the consequences of the introduction of new techniques. Ploughing, for example, by multiplying the productivity of labour, would allow those who at present control the land in theory, to control it in fact. It is not impossible that we should witness what would amount to the appropriation, by certain noble families, of a large part of the village lands. Let us emphasise that this is already the case with the *falo* lands, which are rare and much sought-after. Such lands are generally monopolised by those with hereditary rights.

II STRUCTURE AND FUNCTIONING OF THE FAMILY LANDHOLDINGS

Once again, without claiming an exhaustive analysis, we shall limit ourselves to a few general observations which to us seem important in the context of our objectives.

1. *The continuing cohesion of traditional family structures*

The first and most striking observation is the existence of very large family units (*ka*) containing twenty to thirty people, often even more, living within one common compound. Only a detailed study will allow us to establish whether there is a connection between the size of family groups and membership of a given caste or ethnic group. None the less, it would seem that the phenomenon is as common among the Toucouleur as among the Soninke.

These family communities clearly present a coherent structure, and are not simply cohabitation units. They often contain several matrimonial households (each one made up of a man, his wife or wives, and the children) arranged according to a rigorous hierarchy governed by the principle of primogeniture: the generation of 'fathers' taking precedence over that of 'children'; the older age-groups over the younger ones. The highest authority is in the hands of the head of the *ka*, the *kagumme*, who is either the father (if he is still alive) or the eldest brother.

Within certain limits that require definition, we shall see in the Guidimaka a form of collective organisation based upon the extended family. Although now largely destroyed throughout much of Africa, particularly where it has been integrated into the colonial economy,[3] as a functional unit it still survives in full vitality in the Guidimaka.

2. *Land distribution and the organisation of work*

The family landholding generally consists of several collective plots, *tekhore*, scattered among the different zones of the village land, at least in the case of families who have access to all the lands belonging to the village.

There are also some fields which are still collectively owned, but cultivated by individuals: the plots of the adult men and the young men (*salluma*) are distinguished from those of the women (*yakharinte*). However, we have found some families where only the women worked individual plots, the men working together on the collective fields.

With respect to the organisation of work, the principles are as follows. Each morning, the men go to the collective fields. In the afternoon, the plan is more complicated: individual plots are tilled, but in a sequential manner. Work is organised according to the hierarchy which governs the relationships between individuals within the kinship system. All those who are of lower rank than the head of the household (the *kagumme*) go to work on his fields first; then after a certain time they go on to the field of the head of the next household down, and so on. If there is any time left, the young men are then free to go to work on their own fields.

It should also be noted that quite commonly (on Fridays, the day of prayer, and on Mondays) everyone is free to do as they wish.

These are, of course, theoretical norms. It is difficult to say just how this system is modified in practice. None the less, it is in fairly wide use, and the few examples that we have analysed have indicated this. What is interesting to note is the collective character of the work, even on the individual plots. In emergencies, and for the harvest, the whole family can come together to work the whole of the family landholding — both the collective fields and the individual plots. In addition, we must stress that in certain cases the former slaves of noble families come to give their help.

The *women* (and children) take part in the following work on the collective land: sowing, guarding, harvesting and storing of the grain. Sometimes they may help in the second weeding. Apart from time devoted to housework, they are free to work their own plots. They are usually helped by their husbands with the clearing, sowing and harvesting, and by their children with all their tasks.

3. *Distribution of produce and division of responsibilities*

Here the rules are more confused and there are contradictions within the available data. However, the general principle is as follows (subject to systematic and detailed studies of specific examples):

The family head, who manages the product of the *tekhore*, has the responsibility for meeting the basic needs of the people under his authority: most particularly with regard to food, payment of taxes and the upkeep of their dwellings. In former times he was also responsible for the bride-price to be paid on the marriage of a young man from his *ka*.

The women have to provide only the condiments for the sauce which goes with the couscous or rice dishes (groundnuts, cowpeas, okra, tomatoes). In theory they are free to do as they wish with the produce of their own fields. They may help the family head or their husband, with rice for special feasts, or for welcoming guests, and with sorghum, if the production of the collective fields is insufficient. In any case, their contribution is always considered as a loan.[4] However, as we stressed above, it should be noted that the women are producing more and more sorghum at the expense of their former traditional crops (groundnuts, cotton and indigo). We found the case of one family where the total grain production from the wives' plots was much higher than that from the collective fields. In practice, the women seem to be more and more active in maintaining the subsistence level of the family group. Once personal consumption and gifts have been allowed for, any surplus is either sold, or more usually bartered, for clothes for themselves and their daughters, as well as to make up the marriage endowments of their children.

The norms are less clear when we come to the use of the harvest from the men's individual plots. According to some sources (Bathily, 1969; Pollet and Winter, op.cit.), the younger brothers, or the married sons to whom the family head gives a certain latitude in order to work their own plots, should in return take on a certain number of responsibilities, particularly as regards food. These normally include assistance for the *kagumme* or a guarantee of food for themselves and the members of their household for a certain number of days per week. Our interviews in the villages did not reveal this phenomenon, although it should be remembered that, as individuals, the emigrants do contribute to the support of their families through the regular sending of money.

4. *The effects of migration*

It is clear that, in spite of the apparent persistence of traditional forms of organisation, agricultural production at a family level has undergone some profound changes as a result of the growth of migration. In this respect, two points seem to deserve particular attention.

The first is concerned with the extreme weakening of the labour force available to the family group. This is shown by the active participation in agricultural work of individuals who in normal times would only fulfil a marginal role: young children and old people.[5] However, the labour drain is too strong to be compensated for by this measure, and so we see a large growth in the numbers of agricultural wage-labourers. Thanks to the money sent by the migrants, the family head can take on substitute labour and so maintain family production at a minimum level. This recourse to an outside labour force seems to be a substitution operation, not a process for accumulating labour and, in consequence, wealth.[6]

It is quite significant in this regard that a large part of the workers are employed as 'domestics', which gives them a certain place in the system of family relationships. Housed and fed by their 'boss', they owe him in return three mornings per week. The rest of the time they are paid 50-60 Ouguiyas per day worked. It should be noted, however, that the use of day-labourers is tending to spread, particularly in the villages of the interior after the influx of refugees at the time of the drought.

The growth in numbers of agricultural wage-labourers is an important phenomenon. On the one hand, it is important because of its potential impact upon production relations within local society and their integration into a system of monetarised exchange. On the other hand, such a phenomenon is significant because of the extent to which it places a growing part of agricultural activity on the shoulders of individuals who are outside the family, and often outside the ethnic group, and who for this reason are very little concerned about improvements which could be made in this field. In the general context outlined above, this is undoubtedly an extra factor conducive to stagnation.

The second point has to do with the ever-increasing role of individuals in the running of the family economy. First of all, it is to a large extent thanks to the personal contributions of emigrants that the subsistence of those who have remained in the village is assured through employing outside labour and by buying supplementary food products. As we have seen, although the women theoretically retain control of their production, their contribution is becoming increasingly crucial in maintaining family consumption at a satisfactory level. Furthermore, and without doubt of greatest significance, is the fact that incomes from migration clearly seem to be a way of satisfying individually the aspirations and needs which formerly were the responsibility of the *kagumme*, in his capacity as manager of the family group's collective produce. This is particularly the case with the payment of bride-price, the upkeep and improvement of dwellings and with clothing.

These remarks bring us to question the real meaning of this persistence of traditional family structures. Certainly it is undeniable that in their size, as well as in the communal ways of living and working, the family groups observed in the Guidimaka seem to perpetuate a very old form of organisation. But quite clearly, behind that apparently unchanged facade, the system of economic relationships has been profoundly modified. Whereas before, the destiny of each individual[7] could be fulfilled only within the family group, acting then as the basic unit in the production and distribution of wealth, today it is through an individual search, whose path is traced by emigration, that the young men seek to improve their lot.

In this new context, the operation of the kinship group as a coherent unit (which it still is at the level of daily life and of agricultural activity) becomes a secondary factor in relation to emigration, the dominant force around which the whole of the family economy is polarised. In fact, it is only because of the survival of a collective organisation which ensures the subsistence under satisfactory conditions of those who remain in the village (in particular the women and children), that the migrant can go. Under such an umbrella he can support his family without exposing them to risks that are too great. Thus the family group, in its current form, ensures the safe collective basis which allows individuals to devote themselves to what has become their most important economic activity: emigration.

III THE SYSTEM OF AGRICULTURAL PRODUCTION WITHIN THE REGIONAL AND NATIONAL ECONOMY

1. *Trade*

The most important point in this regard is the low volume of trade involving local agricultural production. A large part of the transfers actually take place within the village community itself. These transfers involve women's production, in particular. The women, as we have just seen, work individual plots. Their produce is often an important contribution to total family production. Part of it is consumed within the *ka*, another part is used as gifts; and finally, the remainder is exchanged outside the *ka*, through sale or barter (millet for groundnuts, for milk, for cowpea leaves, to pay the weaver, etc.).

In other circumstances, particularly in the villages of the interior where emigration is less important, a certain number of farmers find themselves forced to sell millet to cope with unavoidable monetary expenses (until recently, taxes in particular).

Within the rural community itself and by these different ways a certain form of accumulation may occur in the hands of a few wealthy persons: particularly traders and migrants.

There is also a second form of trade, much greater in volume, between different populations or different zones of the Guidimaka region. Thus there are frequent transfers of cereals, sold or bartered, between the farmers and the nomads (Peul or Maure) living in camps near the villages.[8] Maure traders may also bring groundnuts from certain zones of the Senegal river and of the Karakoro (particularly towards Baediam) to exchange for millet in the villages in the north of the region.

Finally, there are a few surviving vestiges of the great traditional trade currents between the Guidimaka and the nomad zones further to the north. By limiting the surpluses available for export from the region, the stagnation of agricultural production has very much lessened the volume of this trade. This year in Selibabi, which has been, for many years, one of the most important centres of this interregional trade, the amount of millet available on the market was extremely small.

Once more, only a specific study would enable us to assess with any accuracy the quantities of agricultural produce, particularly cereals, which are circulating through the different channels we have outlined. What is certain is that the Guidimaka has a potential market much more important and much wider than the one which it is at the moment supplying.[9]

It is, in fact, only in the case of cattle that we can observe any sizeable interregional or international exchanges. We should note that within the Guidimaka the Soninke emigrants, who have a strong tendency to invest in cattle, are on the one hand large buyers from the herders (mainly Peul) but, on the other hand, are rarely sellers.

In recent years, and because of the situation created by the drought, the herders' sales to the slaughterhouse and cold-store at Kaedi have been very large. We should note, however, that these sales have practically ceased since the end of the drought. In Selibabi itself, the annual figure for cattle slaughtered is about 1,000 head per year (estimate from the Animal Husbandry Department at Selibabi).

Finally, until March 1975, the free trading in animals between Mauritania and Senegal favoured a large illicit trade, which has been very difficult to estimate. The official statistics for animals imported from Mauritania were, in Bakel, 3,190 cattle, 82,828 sheep and goats in 1973; and 2,224 cattle, 62,936 sheep and goats in 1974 (estimates from the Animal Husbandry Department at Bakel). But it is certain that these estimates have little to do with reality. Faced with this dangerous 'haemorrhage', the Mauritanian authorities decided in March 1975 to forbid all exports of animals by private individuals.

To conclude this brief review of the situation, we must stress the weakness of the commercial infrastructure in the Guidimaka. Even though the four Maure shops that do exist in Selibabi provide regular supplies of sugar, rice, tea and other basic commodities, this bears no relation at all to the great mass of spending power which the migrants' money now represents (in all, 100 million Ouguiyas per year). For any important purchase — particularly for building materials, of which we know that emigrants consume a great deal — the people have to go to Bakel.[10]

This situation has obviously not come about by chance. It is the direct result of the neglect which this region has suffered for decades. Having nothing to sell except for a little gum arabic, which was usually taken directly to Bakel, it could offer the big commercial houses of Dakar no sufficiently strong incentive to entice them to invest in a buying and distribution network.

It is only since 1960 that this massive influx of money has become a reality, and it was at this time that a century-long pattern of colonial exchange was coming to an end. Despite the considerable profits of the past, capital interests were now turning to alternative and more rewarding investments in other sectors. The commercial sector was being left to small entrepreneurs, who do not have the resources to respond to the new situation created by emigration, nor to benefit from such a source of profit as the potential market of the Guidimaka.[11]

This marginal position in relation to the commercial trading circuits is, we believe, an important fact. It is largely because of it that the Soninke and Toucouleur farmers have been able to escape the mechanisms of domination, the foremost of which is indebtedness, of which these trading exchanges are most often the instruments.

2. *Official support for agricultural production*

The different government departments concerned with agricultural development are represented in Selibabi: Agricultural Services, Animal Husbandry Department, Forestry Department,

Co-operatives Department. However, the inadequacy of the means which are available to the various administrative bodies (lack of staff and vehicles, particularly), the great problems involved in supplying this part of Mauritania (due to its distance from the major axes of communication) and, lastly, the impossibility of travelling in the Guidimaka during the rainy season, are all factors which seriously impede their operations. This is why their impact on local agricultural production and the local economy remains extremely small. The spread of agricultural equipment and modern productive techniques is very slight; it is only in very few villages that equipment for animal traction ploughing is to be found, and in even fewer that those who have it know in fact how to use it. In the field of agriculture the only large-scale operation to have been carried out systematically was the anti-locust campaign (insecticide distribution).[12]

As regards animal husbandry, a programme of vaccination against cattle plague is now in progress: 120,000 doses were given in 1974.

Let us note, finally, the establishment of several co-operatives (vegetable producers at Selibabi, fishermen at Solou and consumer co-operatives at Diogountourou and Diaguili).

To sum up, the results have so far been few, and we may state that in the region as a whole, agricultural and pastoral activities have not benefited up to now from any systematic aid capable of leading to their improvement. This observation is obviously not intended as any reflection on the competence of the administration, nor of the staff of the technical services. Given the lack of financial and material means at their disposal, it is difficult to see how they could have carried out a more effective operation. We should point out in this connection that any project for limited intervention, such as that which will be proposed at the end of this analysis, can have no chance of success unless it receives at a local level, and particularly in the supply and distribution of the factors of production, the support of an adequately efficient infrastructure.

NOTES

1 These are, of course, theoretical rules; in practice, if only because some people practise crop rotation with fallow periods, long-term property rights must tend to become established. It was also pointed out to us that in fact at Diaguili and Moulessimou a symbolic payment had to be made to the village head by any outsiders who wished to cultivate the *dieri*.

2 The locally used measure of volume of grain, roughly equivalent to a bowlful.

3 Thus, about thirty years ago a fairly similar form of family organisation was

observed among the Hausa of Niger and Nigeria; this has now almost completely disappeared (Greenberg, 1946; Raynaut, 1973).

4 But within these limits the family head retains the means of control, so as to reduce sales outside the family as much as possible until a sufficient supply for the needs of the family has been assured.

5 Thus, we found at Diaguili a young boy of 12 or 13 years old playing the role of head of household, working the family fields to provide food for his mother and brothers and sisters.

6 The figures on this point in Kane and Lericollais (op.cit., p.19) are quite revealing: they show that the use of seasonal workers only partially compensates, in general, for the loss to the work-force from the departure of the migrants.

7 This applies both at the level of day-to-day subsistence and at that of achieving the main stages of one's social life — particularly marriage.

8 This is undoubtedly connected with the fact that the nomads often take on work as field-hands in these same villages in order to obtain money.

9 It is none the less interesting to point out the special case of Dafort, whose much appreciated tobacco is consumed all over Mauritania.

10 Even the administration services themselves often have to go to Senegal to buy the supplies they need to keep going: paper, office equipment, petrol (there is no petrol station in Selibabi).

11 We should also stress the inadequacy of the communication infrastructure: only one road remains passable in the rainy season, that from Selibabi to Bakel; the others are simple unmade tracks which even in the dry season can take only a very small amount of traffic. Do we need to underline the close link between this state of affairs and the absence of any economic attractiveness which has characterised the Guidimaka until now?

12 Not forgetting the vegetable-gardens operation carried out by the Agricultural Department, which we gave an account of earlier on.

Conclusion

The very brief duration of our field studies has barely enabled us to proceed beyond a superficial level of analysis. Nevertheless, it is now possible to isolate several facts which to us seem to constitute the principal features determining the system of agricultural production in the Guidimaka: the major themes of the diagnosis, on the basis of which we shall be able to suggest a number of precise proposals for action which combine to form a coherent project.

The essential features of this diagnosis may be summarised as follows:

(1) *The weak role of market mechanisms in the internal functioning of the local economy, and the marginal place of agricultural production activities within the general system of colonial exploitation.*

In comparison with the impact of commodity exchange in societies closely involved with the groundnut economy, the resistance of Soninke society to the penetration of monetary exchange has been striking. Clearly, barter remains active, even though it involves relatively limited quantities of produce. Millet, groundnuts, cowpeas, milk and cloth circulate daily in this way within the village community. It is also quite common for similar forms of exchange to occur between farmers and herders (millet for the herders' produce), and between farmers and Maure traders (millet for salt, sugar and groundnuts).

In general, sale or barter transactions such as these involve only a very small part of local agricultural production. In the riverine villages it is rare for a family head to sell cereals. It is only the *falo* crops (especially pumpkins, calabashes and sweet potatoes) which are systematically marketed. In the interior it appears that the poorest farmers (particularly those who have no migrants in the family) are often obliged to sell millet. However, small quantities are involved and sales take place only when forced by necessity. Other, specialised crops, such as tobacco from Dafort, may be regularly traded.

Money may also circulate through wage-labour, which, as we have seen, is becoming common practice in the Guidimaka.

However, those who are employed as day-labourers or 'domestics' rarely belong to local peasant communities. In most cases they are migrants either from Mali (in the riverine villages) or Peul or Harratine Maure (in the villages of the interior).

Moreover, when we consider that transactions involving land are extremely rare, we see that the phenomenon of 'commercialisation' has so far had very little effect upon socio-economic relationships within the local society. To a great extent, therefore, relationships within the community are still governed by norms from which the concept of profit is absent; this remains true also in respect of the principal factor of production, land.

Obviously, such a situation is closely linked to the fact that profit can be more viably obtained through the external source of migration than through the internal functioning of the local economy. This is important from the point of view of the degree to which social structures have been able to maintain cohesion. In particular, we should emphasise the absence of inegalitarian mechanisms founded on the commercial appropriation of land and labour. As we have seen, wage-labour seems to act more as a means for compensating the loss of labour through emigration than as a means of accumulating a labour force and increasing wealth.

Certainly, large monetary flows exist within the community, but they have developed in a separate circuit, parallel to the internal social and economic relationships of the society. Through the purchase of manufactured goods or imported foodstuffs, externally derived money mostly returns to the outside without affecting the working of the local system of agricultural production. It neither disturbs it, since the most important factor in the organisation of production and the distribution of produce is still the family structure, nor does it add any dynamic force, since the purchasing power represented by money from emigration has been little used to improve local agricultural production.[1] If there is any active mechanism by which wealth may be accumulated, it is certainly at the level of this 'parallel' circulation of money that it is to be observed. Traders and 'men of confidence', often one and the same person, are doubtless the foci around which such a concentration occurs. However, we have no precise data of this phenomenon, and we can do no more than hypothesise.

Three main consequences arise from these facts:

(a) *Stagnation in the local agricultural production system*
We have stated many times in the preceding analysis that, if we wish to understand the present situation in the Guidimaka, the dominant factor of migration must be acknowledged (be it from

the economic, social or agricultural point of view). The harmful effects of this 'human haemorrhage' are innumerable and we have indicated only a few of them. Nevertheless, because of its very isolation, the region has escaped the strong tendency of economic and social structures to disintegration which characterises those areas that were of more interest to colonial capitalism. Such a disintegration is manifest in the over-exploitation of land through the pursuit of excessive yields, the destruction of agrarian systems, the break-up of family groups and farming units, the strangulation of producers by debt, and their super-exploitation through the multiple mechanisms of surplus extraction (particularly at the level of the commercialisation of their agricultural production).

By contrast, the experience in the villages of the Guidimake has been one of a general withdrawal of their agricultural production system. This is witnessed both in the contraction of its range of activities (some traditional crops showing a significant decline), and in the shrinkage of the area of utilised land (some zones of the landholdings being progressively abandoned).

One can see in these changes the effects of the recent years of drought, although this offers only a partial explanation. Most certainly, the determinant factor is still emigration. In so far as the latter has come to dominate economic and social life, it has forced agriculture into a lesser role: that of ensuring the subsistence of those who remain in the village. However, even this minimal function is not totally assured. To an increasing extent, food consumption is becoming dependent on external produce, despite the fact that the most important commodities, such as rice, vegetable oil, and tomato sauce, can be produced in the region, given suitable investment. Thus, we see that the present situation is characterised by a lethargy in the agricultural production system — a lethargy against which no vigorous initiative in agricultural development has been counteractive. A complement of this lethargy is an increasing reliance on the exterior for the whole of economic life.

(b) *The preservation of the potential of the natural environment and of the possibilities for agricultural development*

With the exception of a few, localised examples of limited environmental degradation, which are linked to the effects of the recent drought, from the point of view of natural environmental potential, it is certain that the overall situation in the Guidimaka is still favourable.

Precisely because of agricultural stagnation in recent decades, considerable areas of land are still available, soil fertility is generally good, and disturbance of the ecological balance is localised. Although we must recognise that this equilibrium is fundamentally fragile, and that in dealing with such an environment caution is necessary, the general prospects for the development of agricultural production are extremely positive.

(c) *The maintenance of a certain degree of social cohesion*
In response to the needs generated by the growth of migration, but also as a result of the fact that within the system of agricultural production social relations have been very little infected by 'commercialisation', a high degree of social cohesion continues to exist within local society, particularly amongst the Soninke. Their forms of collective organisation remain very strong, both at the village level (witnessed by the establishment of associations and funds for mutual aid), and at the family level (through the persistence of extended family groupings).

Even with such a foundation, we must not overestimate the possibility of building communal work structures. Nevertheless, the existence of village groundnut fields near the river, the success of collective vegetable gardens initiated by the Secteur Agricole, the enthusiasm with which several villages on the Senegalese bank have undertaken important collective tasks (rainy-season cropping over several hectares, vegetable gardening, and the development of rice perimeters),[2] seem to indicate that, in so far as projected activities are related to precise objectives and do not provoke competition between participants, it is possible to envisage proposing to local farmers a strategy of action which requires collective effort.

The confirmation of such a hypothesis is seen in local village communities, where an extremely strong social control encourages collective decision-making and implementation. We may illustrate this by the example of one village in the Guidimaka, where the village council undertook in 1975 to fix the price of millet at a very low level, so as to discourage the producers from selling their reserves. Anyone contravening this decision was to be punished by a fine. This is a crucial point, since it leads us to think that such strongly organised social communities would be capable of deciding on technical and economic matters of quite wide application; in fact, of formulating a development strategy for the whole village.

(2) *The need to consider the process of agricultural production, and the improvements that may possibly be instituted, in terms of a system*

It has become obvious to us that the agricultural practices of the peasant communities of the region form a coherent functional whole, whose constituent parts are closely interlinked and in equilibrium. In particular, we have shown the ways in which both complementarity and contradiction exist, and which are apparent both in the realisation of the different potential of each environmental zone, and in the allocation of agricultural tasks over time. In this respect each village is a special case, with its own environmental conditions and degree of labour shortage. These may be advantageous to the production process or may, on the other hand, result in bottlenecks.

In the context of an agricultural development project, the use of new techniques, crops and varieties must not be introduced via a standard, 'package' extension programme, but as a function of the solutions that they will offer within a complex equilibrium. Intervention must seek to resolve certain contradictions, to unblock specified bottlenecks, and so to arrive at an overall improvement in the level of agricultural production.

Thus, in a village where the tightness of the agricultural calendar and the labour competition between operations in different parts of the land systems are the principal limiting factors, the introduction of techniques which reduce work-time (fungicides to increase germination success and obviate the replacements of lost seedlings, weeding with animal traction, etc.) could significantly alleviate the situation. Elsewhere, a zone whose potential is under-used because of a lack of adequate technical means, such as an area of *fonde* which could be put under irrigated gardening, would require a different approach. Such a *fonde* zone will only be effectively used if operations do not compete in the agricultural calendar with time needed for other crops on a different type of land. In such a case, the provision of techniques which allow time to be gained in the cultivation of these other crops would be the indispensable precondition for the introduction of such an improvement. Finally, there are cases where the introduction of a new crop, although desired by farmers, would come into competition with a traditional and more important crop such as sorghum, because of demands on the same land. It is obvious that in such a case a substantial improvement in the yields of the preferred crop is again the indispensable precursor to the introduction of the new variety.

The cohesion within an agricultural system is such that an action plan of any significance cannot be undertaken in any one sector of it without taking into account its repercussions on all its other parts.

This brief analysis permits the identification of the major themes for the formulation of a rural development project, adapted to the specific conditions of the Guidimaka, which can be summed up as follows:

The concern of the project will not focus on farming units as distinct individual 'enterprises' (in order to improve their technical and economic 'rationality'), but rather on the agro-economic systems taken as coherent and functional wholes. It is the relationship of the rural community as a whole to its natural and economic environment which requires improvement.

The positive aspects which characterise the present marginal position of the agricultural system of the Guidimaka will have to be made use of. To this end, it will be essential to promote initially a type of development aimed at reinforcing the autonomy of the rural communities, that is, a strengthening of the technical and economic bases of agricultural production. This will be achieved

(i) by endeavouring primarily to satisfy the basic food requirements (thereby reducing the importance of monetary exchanges for food imported to the area),

(ii) by advocating those technical improvements which require the lowest possible financial investments.

In view of this diagnosis and of the strategic guidelines outlined above, it is now possible to define the main orientations of an agricultural development project.

MAIN ORIENTATIONS

It would be unrealistic to think of agriculture as an alternative to migration in the short term. Considering the combination of the low yields and low product prices, it is difficult to see how returns from any agricultural production that could be envisaged now could compete, even partially, with the income to be obtained by going to France.

Of course, migration is not in any sense a long-term solution, and everything must be done to enable the younger generation in the Guidimaka to find a local production activity which ensures a satisfactory livelihood. But this is a long-term objective which can only be achieved through several stages. To reach this goal it is clear that the transition to commercial agriculture must occur. But under what conditions is important. The consequences of the complete integration of peasant societies into the market economy are well known from elsewhere: the loss of all control over their agricultural production (the development of which takes place in response to pressures exerted from the exterior and not as a function of their own needs), the disruption of the subsistence production system, increased dependence on the exterior, the emergence of real impoverishment.

It has been the mixed privilege of the farmers of the Guidimaka to remain outside this evolution. The task to be undertaken now is to help reorganise and consolidate their position in such a way that the development of a market sector in their economy (capable of becoming an alternative solution to migration) can be brought about to their advantage and not at their expense.

Reorganising and consolidating their position means essentially:
— improving their mastery of the agricultural production system;
— ensuring security and independence in all that concerns the satisfaction of their essential needs (particularly for food).

By 'mastery of the production system' is meant the capacity to:
— understand the overall functioning of the system, including its equilibrium, the internal contradictions, its constraints and potentialities;
— establish production objectives which arise from a conscious choice in response to perceived needs;
— determine the necessary activities to improve the production system to achieve the chosen objectives.

This implies the necessary existence in each village of a collective organisation for analysis and decision-making which would have the responsibility for designing this type of village 'micro-plan' and for controlling its implementation.

By ensuring the 'security and independence' is meant to:
— direct primary effort to the improvement of subsistence crops to ensure their abundant and regular supply;
— ensure that where possible both production and processing are done locally (diversification of crops, and development of processing skills).

It is only on the basis of a production system organised along these lines and focused on the needs of the peasant communities that the transition to an economy which is more fully open to market exchange can occur. With this perspective, it is necessary, at the outset, to encourage at the regional level possible complementarities in production between zones with different specialisations.

The success of such a programme rests fundamentally on the

possibility of achieving a global improvement in the village agricultural system. In concrete terms this implies:

1. Improving the securing of agricultural production in view of the extreme environmental variability, especially through:
   — the use of improved crop varieties;
   — the increased efficiency of water usage;
   — disease control in crops and livestock.

2. Increasing the productivity of agriculture, especially through:
   — encouraging the improvement of traditional agricultural techniques by the introduction of simple, low-cost and appropriate technologies (varietal selection, crop rotation, use of organic manure, soil preparation, treatment of harvested crops);
   — introducing, where necessary, modern technical tools (ploughing, pumps).

3. Taking the best advantage of the potential of the natural environment by:
   — giving the farmers the technical means of exploiting all of the agricultural land they used to cultivate, in particular, the higher, sandy areas. This implies in particular the reduction of labour-time among the different crops to reduce the bottlenecks which exist at present;
   — the establishment of hydro-agricultural projects which allow the exploitation of land until now either unused or inefficiently used (the use of ponds and depressions, irrigation of areas of the *fonde* beside the river).

4. Taking the best advantage of the significant capital represented by the cattle herds:
   — developing disease-control projects already in progress;
   — improving the techniques of herd management (selection, feeding);
   — assuring a positive integration of agriculture and livestock (using animal traction and animal manure, the production of fodder and other feed for cattle).

These strategies, which are directed towards returning to the village production system and the dynamism it now lacks, will be implemented largely through a redirection of the money coming from emigration. This can occur through two main channels:

— the undertaking of both collective and individual investments wherever possible;
— the use of the purchasing power of this money to develop increased consumption of local production, particularly with new crops (vegetables, fruit, wheat) or those which are little grown at present.

The entire strategy which has been briefly outlined must respect two basic principles at the level of its implementation:

1. To minimise the disturbance and degradation of the fragile natural environment.
2. To strive towards the least inegalitarian distribution within the rural community of both the factors of production and the fruits of production. To reduce as much as possible the risks in this regard, activities should be orientated mainly towards collective organisation. It will be necessary, however, to avoid imposing rigid structures, but to encourage, on the contrary, the establishment of varied groups whose composition and size will allow, in each case, the best compatibility with the technical and economic demands of the strategy, but also with existing affiliations within each village.

NOTES

1   With the exception of the heavy investments in cattle, which constitute an important reorientating of the system of production.
2   Within the framework of the 'development project' managed by CIDR.

PART III
Rural Development Project Proposed in the 10th Region

CHAPTER 12

The Project

I THE PROJECT AREA

It is certain that the most urgent action is needed in the north-east of the Guidimaka, in particular the villages at the foot of the Assaba Massif. The instability of the natural environment and the greater dependence of the peasant communities on agriculture make urgent action necessary.

However, given that an extensive development plan is anticipated within the medium term for the whole of the south-east of Mauritania, and that it will affect all the areas in which dry-farming is predominant, it seems preferable to direct War on Want's intervention towards the riverine areas which will not be affected by this scheme.

The project proposed here will encompass the following villages: Khabou, Solou, Diogountourou, Moulessimou, Diaguili, Gouraye, Lexelba, Betselba, Woumpou, Takoutala, as well as several small settlements within this area.

Given the data at our disposal, we estimate the total population involved at 11,150, of whom about 9,000 are Soninke and 2,500 are Toucouleur and Peul.

The total area will be covered in two stages:

(i) In the first stage (two years) the project will cover the villages of Solou, Diogountourou, Moulessimou, Diaguili, Gouraye, Lexelba, Betselba, representing a total population of 6,750.

(ii) In the second stage, the intervention will also include the villages of Khabou, Woumpou, Takoutala and also the smaller settlements, an added population of about 4,400.

II THE PROGRAMME OF ACTION

1. *The Social Framework for Technical Activities*

The formation of collective organisations, which would form the framework within which the envisaged technical activities could be implemented, is a fundamental component of the project. The impact and significance of technical innovations are a function of the context in which they are implemented; that is to say, the economic objectives which determine their selection, and the nature of the social units which fix those objectives and are involved in their implementation.

In no way is our aim to impose the establishment of structures of communal production. That is a choice that can be made only by the peasant communities themselves, and within the framework of a national policy. What is really sought is:

(i) The co-ordination of production activities at a sufficiently broad level (the village) to allow the definition and pursuance of objectives which are wide enough to allow the consideration of new perspectives to agricultural production.

(ii) The easier, more rapid and more extensive diffusion of new technical knowledge (in order that all those who are interested actually have access to the information).

(iii) The possible concentration of labour-power (eventually of capital) on the achievement of tasks which are of collective interest.

This organisation will be effected at several levels.

(a) *Village associations*
As of right, every member of the village community will belong to these. A management and an executive committee will be chosen in a manner decided by the villagers themselves.

The establishment of these associations will meet the following objectives:

— To allow the widest possible participation by the village community in defining the programme of actions to be implemented in each locality affected by the project.
— To establish at the village level a structure to co-ordinate and control the implementation of actions considered desirable.
— To ensure the existence in each village of an organisation responsible for the management of the funds available for carrying out the programme of action.

Thus, the basic function of these associations will be to elaborate a micro-plan of agricultural development which is adapted to the realities, the problems and the needs of each village, and to ensure the control and co-ordination of its implementation.

Their first task will be to collect, with the help of the project staff, the necessary information to establish objectives and to determine an appropriate plan of action for each village. Such information includes existing constraints in the production system, particularly the natural environment and the availability of labour, and the expressed needs of the village community in terms of agricultural products.

On the basis of the information gathered, there must then be a collective reflection and analysis to isolate the areas where solutions are most urgently needed, notably, the identification of both the bottlenecks in the production process and of those crops whose production needs to be improved or which could be introduced.

Based on the results of this reflection, the next stage is to put in motion a programme to seek technical solutions, which is carried out by the peasants themselves in a way to be defined below. Within this programme it will be possible to test technical innovations which may provide solutions to the identified problems.

From the results of this programme, the village associations will be able to select, on the basis of their efficiency and suitability for solving the problems, a number of themes for an extension programme. The associations will co-ordinate and control this extension programme, which will be carried out according to a plan defined below.

As the practices and techniques improve, the village associations will take measures to co-ordinate production at the level of the whole village, to make it respond more closely to the identified needs. These might include the development of crops that are either not cultivated or little cultivated at present, and when the general level of the traditional crops has been improved, specific projects, such as the cultivation of specific zones in the land system, could be considered. The village associations will ensure the management and distribution of the funds which will be given to each village, as part of a programme of annual activity, and within the context of each village project. It is the associations which will assume the responsibility for the utilisation of these funds. This will be the beginning of a 'village budget' whose financing will be able to fall partially, and progressively to a greater extent as the project develops, on to the participants themselves.

It must be noted that the whole of the process described above will take place continuously. As the more basic objectives are achieved, more ambitious plans can be conceived, tried out and implemented. As has been suggested in the 'Main Orientation', the long-term objective of this continuous and coherent plan can be to enable, through an improvement in the traditional production system which is based on subsistence, the development of a market sector in agricultural production. This is important because it is only through sufficiently motivating prospects for the future that the farmers will undertake the modification of the relatively static equilibrium of their present production system, however modest the characteristics of the actions at the beginning of the project.

136

(b) *Collective fields, as experimentation plots and demonstration areas*

It is on a collective basis that activities concerning the introduction of new agricultural practices will be carried out; the trying out of new technical tools, new crop varieties and new cultivated areas. The research programme which is defined at the level of the village associations will be carried out by groups of farmers working on collective fields. This will be under the direction of the associations and with the continuing assistance of the project staff.

These fields will consist of several plots in different cultivated zones. They must be representative, particularly from the pedological point of view, and situated so as to offer easy access to the villagers. The area of these fields must be small enough not to impose too heavy a burden on the members of the groups working on them, and not to conflict with working on their own land.

When certain agricultural practices or technical innovations have been judged relevant by the village associations, some of the plots can serve as demonstration areas.

The advantage of such collective organisation lies in the wide participation it allows by the villagers themselves in the concrete operations of discussing, selecting and demonstrating the themes which will be proposed for the extension programme. The project staff must make sure that they leave the maximum of responsibility for the practical execution of the programme with the groups involved. Furthermore, a continuing collective evaluation must be encouraged, so as to develop the farmers' capacity to assess the true possibilities for applying, within the framework of the private family fields, the techniques being tested. The existence of several plots will play an essential role from this point of view, because it will allow the identification of possible competing demands for either time or space in agricultural operations.

The links between the groups responsible for the collective fields and the village associations will develop in two directions. It will be the associations who will decide the programme of activities and supervise their execution; further, the results obtained on the collective fields and the evaluation carried out by the groups must be reported, analysed and discussed within the associations. This is to ensure the best possible spread of information and the selection of techniques and technical inputs which will be suitable for the extension programme.

Livestock management could give rise to a similar organisation. The working out of the directions for technical improvement and their demonstration could be done through a small collective herd, whose management would be undertaken by a specific group.

Collaboration between the two forms of activity (agricultural and pastoral) must be constant, so as to encourage the closest possible co-operation between agriculture and livestock management.

(c) *Organisation of the extension programme*

A first stage in the extension programme can take place through the collective fields based on the demonstration plots. None the less, a more thorough evaluation of the new techniques and their wider diffusion among the village population will demand a systematic approach and an appropriate extension structure.

To this end, the formation of groups of farmers who work on contiguous plots of land, and who would be interested in practising certain techniques which have been tried out on the collective fields and recognised as relevant by the village association, may be desirable. These groups could be formed around either one of the members of the group working on the collective fields, or any other particularly competent farmer. This farmer would thus serve the function of 'peasant extension worker'. This should not be seen as a rigid form of organisation, as other types of groupings, such as those founded on personal affinities or on age-groups, could serve the same function.

Contiguity of their plots would allow better monitoring of the conditions for the application of selected techniques, the co-ordination of activities, and, eventually, the communal undertaking of certain tasks which need a concentration of labour, particularly those of soil management.

The formation of the group will ensure the circulation of information among individuals who confront the same problems, through the continuous discussion of their successes, their failures and the difficulties which they encounter. This should encourage a much wider diffusion of technical knowledge, without resulting in training 'leaders' or 'model farmers', but raising the average technical level of all the farmers.

There must also be regular discussions at the level of village associations to allow an exchange of the experiences acquired by the different groups, and an overall evaluation of the development of the village production system. In this way it would become possible to establish gradually a co-ordination of agricultural activities at a much wider level, and so be able to establish overall production objectives.

If a particular difficulty made it necessary, technical assistance could be offered directly to these groups by the project staff. However, generally, the work of advising and of extension should fall on the members of the group which works the collective fields,

138

and on farmers who have a good mastery of the techniques to be popularised.

Thus, the complete organisational model which has been presented has different integral levels. It is the 'village associations' which will 'crown' the whole and ensure the co-ordination and the monitoring of the tasks undertaken by specific groups. It is the associations which will have the function of distributing the available funds among the groups and which, in the final analysis, will take the responsibility for the use of the funds.

We must stress that, apart from the overall structure which has been outlined, it will be possible to set up other types of groups as a function of the needs presented by the implementation of the village development plan. Such needs could be the setting-up of irrigated gardens, or of small hydro-agricultural projects, which would also be directed, co-ordinated and controlled by the village association.

Finally, we should note that as soon as there emerges the possibility of a significant modification of the direction and the level of village production, there will have to be co-ordination between the different villages involved in the project. There will have to be exchanges of information and common reflection at an inter-village level, as soon as the need is felt. This will be within a framework and methodology that will have to be defined by the appropriate administrative authorities.

2. Possibilities for improvement of agriculture and livestock management: themes for extension

It is clear that only through the introduction of new technical inputs (in the form of knowledge, crops and tools) can any major improvement in production be made. This is where the value of the framework of social organisation which has been outlined becomes obvious, because the technical efficiency of the plans envisaged is a direct function of the existence and functioning of that framework.

As was stated many times in the course of our multi-disciplinary study, each village operates an agricultural production system which is characterised by a certain number of specific problems. The improvement of the conditions of the agricultural production system cannot, under these conditions, be envisaged as resulting from the systematic application of a certain number of preconceived technical solutions. There is no question, in the context of this project, of proposing a standard 'technological package' which is suggested, *a priori*, to be valid for every situation. It is the opposite strategy which will be adopted. New technical inputs will be introduced only after the particular problems of each particular case have been identified, and after it has been decided by those who experience those problems that the innovations will be likely to provide an effective solution. Selection will be made with reference to criteria that are wider than pure agronomics: any change envisaged will be introduced only after taking into consideration the overall equilibrium of the agricultural system.

Without prejudice either to the flexibility demanded by the diversity of individual cases or to the responsibility for choice which will fall on the village associations, a certain number of guiding principles for agricultural and for livestock management can now be established.

(a) *Agriculture*
The general perspective should be one of progression by stages, starting with a reinforcement of the traditional subsistence system and continuing with the broadening of subsistence production to include those foodstuffs which are currently consumed, but which are either not produced or only produced in small amounts. This eventually leads to the possibility of production for the market (cf. 'Main Orientation'). The project proposed here envisages only the first two stages. The prospect of the third stage should, however, be kept constantly in the background, since it ultimately gives significance to efforts directed at improving the subsistence system.

Initially, efforts should be directed at the selection of simple, low-cost techniques, which would not imply any radical changes in the current system, but which could bring some improvement, even a modest one, to the yields, the security and productivity of labour. As soon as a certain number of such techniques have been recognised, everything must be done (as described above) to ensure their widest possible diffusion within the village community, the principal objective being to improve by stages the average level of agricultural production.

As the simpler techniques become assimilated, the activities of implementation and evaluation can be directed gradually towards more elaborate and, eventually, more costly techniques.

At an advanced stage, when the limit of improvement from simpler techniques has been reached, it will be possible to envisage the opportunity for activities which demand a fairly high level of investment and technology.

On the basis of the results of our field study, it is possible to suggest a few areas where the activities of investigation, adaptation and evaluation could be fruitful.

Agricultural practices. The effectiveness with which the rain and the floodwater are utilised is recognised as low. Taking into account the limitations imposed by the instability of the environment, certain improvements in agricultural practices could noticeably increase the efficiency of water utilisation. Thus, infiltration is reduced by the existence of surface crusts, as well as by the structure of the soil profile. The loss of useful water could be considerably reduced by such practices as:

— reducing and slowing down surface run-off;
— improving infiltration;
— increasing the soil's permeability, its water-retention capacity, and so encouraging root development.

Simple technical achievements in this field could have a considerable impact on agricultural production, from the point of view of both yields and security. The adaptation and diffusion of agricultural practices which alleviate this type of problem therefore seem to be particularly desirable.

In association with an increased efficiency of water-utilisation, improvements in the maintenance and reconstitution of soil fertility could bring significant results. Simple techniques, particularly the use of animal manure (of which large quantities are available) rotation of crops and green manure need to be investigated.

The introduction of new varieties. Within the complex structure of the agricultural environment and within the agricultural system itself, there is a very large potential for improving existing varieties by the introduction of new genetic material. There exists a need for new varieties which are better adapted to the climatic constraints as well as to the different types of soils. The selection of new varieties should be based on the objectives of increased security of production, with the increased capacity to respond to improvements in soil fertility, at the same time as responding to the availability of water. By examining the differences in vegetative cycles which exist between the different varieties, it should also be possible to try to adjust the agricultural calendar and to reduce certain bottlenecks.

Through the use of new varieties which are more drought-resistant, the re-establishment of certain crops which are at the moment in the process of being abandoned could be considered, particularly groundnuts. In response to both the farmers' desire to vary their diet (vegetables and fruit) and their need for independence in the field of basic foodstuffs (cereals), the introduction of new crops could be considered, with the aim of diversifying agricultural production.

Whether introduced through the family fields or through special perimeters (as with wheat and paddy rice), it is clear that the large-scale use of new varieties and crops cannot be envisaged without careful testing. This will evaluate not only their adaptation to the demands of the environment and the overall agricultural system, but also the extent to which they suit the true needs and tastes of the consumers.

The use of new technology. Our analysis has shown that one of the principal limiting factors in agricultural production in the Guidimaka was the lack of an available labour force, as a consequence of emigration. A number of agricultural innovations will certainly demand a considerably increased outlay of labour if they are seen to be applicable on a large scale. The introduction of new tools which could improve the efficiency of labour could then be considered. New tools could be sought for such tasks as the preparation of the soil, and weeding. It should be borne in mind that growth in the productivity of labour at a given point in the agricultural calendar could mean the appearance of bottlenecks at another point. This could occur with the preparation of an area of land that was too large in relation to the time and labour that would be available for weeding. The misuse of the plough could produce such a result. The introduction of these tools should therefore be undertaken with the greatest of care, and only when the limit of improvements that are possible within the framework of traditional technology has been reached. A careful evaluation of their efficiency, their viability and their possible effects on the equilibrium of the natural environment must be made on the collective fields before their inclusion in any extension programme.

The production of forage. In the context of the reinforcement of co-operation between agriculture and livestock management, the production of forage could be desirable. In so far as the general efficiency of the agricultural production system increases, leaving an available surplus of time and space, the production of forage for the local cattle can become practicable. Improvements from this point of view could be achieved in two ways:

(i) the cultivation of species that could be used either directly or indirectly as forage;

(ii) the improvement of natural pastures, for example, by introducing or encouraging certain preferred grasses.

We wish to stress again that all activity relating to the adaptation and evaluation of technical innovations must be thought of as leading to their widest possible application by the village community as a whole. The extension programme, which operates through the groups outlined above, must therefore be the final objective of any search for technical solutions.

(b) *Livestock management*
Cattle are an important potential source of wealth in the areas which will be affected by the project. It is of primary importance to ensure their best possible use. This implies particularly an increase in the resources in kind (milk and meat) as well as in income from the cattle. It means also a closer co-operation between agriculture and livestock management (the use of animal traction, manure, etc.).

Possible activities are:
— the improvement of feeding through the regeneration and better utilisation of natural pasture and experiments with forage crops (see above);
— a beginning to the selection of cattle to improve the herds, particularly from the point of view of using their labour;
— a general improvement in the management of the herd;
— a systematic vaccination programme.

3. *Specific production activities*
Parallel to the activities of the adaptation and extension programme, which is aimed at a general improvement in traditional crops, a number of specific activities can be undertaken to ensure the provision of foodstuffs which either are of low production at present, or are not produced, and whose cultivation demands the establishment of a special infrastructure, for example, with irrigation.

(a) *Fruit and Vegetable Gardening*
The growing of fruit and vegetables under irrigation is included in this category. If the need for greater variety in the diet, especially by the regular consumption of fruit and vegetables, is thought by the village associations to be sufficiently strong to justify a specific action, then this is the type of project which could be undertaken reasonably quickly and which, without demanding an excessive concentration of work and investment, could have significant effects in improving the living conditions of the village communitites.

Where the creation of an irrigated garden-plot is seriously considered, it could be established initially as one of the plots on the collective fields. However, even at this level, it will be characterised by the fact that the central objective of the operation will be not so much the preparation for a technical extension programme, as the direct production of foodstuffs judged necessary, given the consumption needs of the villagers.

As the cultivation techniques are improved, and as more appropriate varieties are found, the irrigated garden-plot, while remaining a collective undertaking, could become an autonomous activity and be gradually extended until it meets the village needs as far as is possible.

The sale of vegetable and fruit produce within the village will be able to create a partial outlet for the purchasing power available within the village community, and so encourage the investment of a part of the money in circulation in production activity (the self-financing of the irrigated garden-plot itself, for example).

At a more advanced stage — given, of course, that the corresponding skills for processing were developing — we could envisage the extension of tomato cultivation and the manufacture of tomato paste, which currently is important in the preparation of local dishes. Such an operation could make a significant contribution to reducing the dependence on outside sources of food.

(b) *Rice cultivation*

Rice has been grown in the project villages for a long time. The first activities envisaged in this area are concerned, therefore, with the gradual improvement in traditional techniques, by the methods presented above, the adaptation of techniques and their extension. However, as the objective is to achieve a growing self-sufficiency in this cereal, more specific and more intensive production activities may be envisaged.

The technical input which is central to these activities is the mastery of water.

— Initially, this can be attempted in some of the *walo* basins through simple and low-cost activities. The variety used would be rainfed rice, grown in the water that is retained as the flood retreats. Thus, this would be an extra refinement of the traditional techniques, allowing more advantage to be taken of the potential resources of the environment.

— In a second stage, if the village development plan made the need apparent and if continuing investigations show its technical feasibility, the irrigation of *fonde* perimeters could be undertaken. The variety grown would be paddy rice, which demands a strict control of water. It is obvious that such large projects with a capability for improving independence from the exterior for food, can be envisaged only when the reinforcement of traditional subsistence cultures is sufficiently advanced.

(c) *Wheat cultivation*
The high current consumption of wheat-flour, as bread, suggests that local production of this cereal could become desirable. If it is desired by village associations and if it is seen to be technically and economically feasible, wheat could be introduced on the *fonde* perimeters beside the paddy rice. Obviously, this would demand the parallel establishment of small mills to produce flour.

This list of specific production activities is not, of course, definitive. As a function of the needs and potential of the different villages, other similar activities may appear desirable. It will be up to the village associations, with the assistance of the project staff, to evaluate their feasibility and to plan their implementation, so as to avoid any competition with the central objective of reinforcing the traditional production system.

4. *The development of craft industries*

Although it is not possible to outline in detail what these should be, it should be taken for granted that the promotion of craft skills should be sought in parallel with that of the agricultural activities. It is indeed one of the essential conditions for the reinforcement of independence from the exterior and a revival of the village economy.

The development of craft skills could occur in several directions:
— the processing of agricultural produce into foodstuffs, for example tomato purée, vegetable oil and flour milling.
— the upkeep and, where possible, the manufacture of new technical tools — carts, for example.
— the production and maintenance of household goods for the improvement of living conditions. Here there is a real possibility of using the technical skills which are acquired by some of the migrants during their stay in France. This is an asset which must not be neglected.

For the establishment of a development programme for crafts and skills, a specific mission of investigation could be undertaken according to the demands expressed by the village associations.

It is probable that the Sahel fund of War on Want will not be able to finance the full implementation of the development programme which has been sketched out. It is none the less impossible to present a clear temporal division into successive stages, each with its own well-defined limits. Indeed, on the other hand it is difficult to foresee what will be the actual rhythm of progress of the activities envisaged; and on the other, it would be contrary to the basic perspective of this project to try and anticipate the choices which are to be made by the village associations.

We can say, however, that it is after a period of five years, which is the foreseeable duration of the project, that the essentials will have been achieved, with the formation of social groups for decision-making, for planning, for technical evaluation and for the extension programmes. Furthermore, the reinforcement of the traditional production system will be well under way and the average level of efficiency of agricultural techniques will have been noticeably raised. We may say, therefore, that a great step will have been taken on the road to a true mastery by the peasants of the overall production system, and the basis for them to take true advantage of larger and more costly technical projects will be assured.

That being the situation, the financing of those actions which will not have been able to be achieved within the framework of this project should not pose any serious problem.

CHAPTER 13

Implementation Procedures

The previous chapters ('Main Orientations', Part II, Section C, and 'The Rural Development Project Proposed in the 10th Region', Part III, Chapter 1) constitute the core of the document submitted to the Government of Mauritania in the autumn of 1975. In the agreement reached in February 1976 between the Government and War on Want, it is clearly stated that both parties endorse the objectives and implementation procedures of the project as set out in the above document, which will be the basis for reference in the event of any alterations to the original project.

STATUS OF THE PROJECT

The project is regarded as an 'autonomous development programme' with its own resources (staff, finances, logistics, and administration), pursuing the objectives agreed by the Government and War on Want, subject to regular evaluation by both parties.

Moreover, the 'project Director', responsible for approving expenditure and a six-monthly work plan, is an official appointed by the Government. The project staff (the 'project Manager' and his 'assistant', both Mauritanian) are responsible to the 'Director' and War on Want, but are not part of the government administration. War on Want, represented by its support and evaluation team, is responsible to the Government and the village communities concerned for ensuring that the project pursues the stated objectives and for the activities undertaken by the project staff.

FINANCIAL MANAGEMENT

War on Want will provide approximately £200,000 over a period of five and a half years to meet the operational costs of the project.

One third of this amount will be allocated to the activities of evaluation, research and assistance to planning carried out by the support and evaluation team representing War on Want. The remainder will be divided between the operational costs of the project (staff salaries and expenses) and the 'village budgets'.

These budgets are an original feature of the project; among other things, it will be the responsibility of the 'village associations' to decide on the use of an annual budget made available to them by the project, and to manage these funds. The use of these resources will be made following a village 'micro-plan' once the collective decision-making structure has determined those activities essential for meeting the objectives of the project.

The yearly amount allocated to each 'village budget' is obviously fairly limited, and can in no way be regarded even as an approximation of the financial requirements necessary for meeting all the problems of agricultural production experienced by the communities. As mentioned previously, the availability of these funds to a collective village body is only the starting-point of a larger process of pooling village resources to be utilised in the collective interest.

THE PROJECT STAFF

Two major factors were taken into account in selecting the Mauritanian staff for the local level:
  (i) national resources in terms of technically trained personnel,
  (ii) the tasks to be carried out in a project of this nature.

(i) Assuming that the ultimate value of an experiment in agricultural development lies in its potential replication on a larger scale (regional or national), we sought as far as possible to equip our project with means that appeared compatible with the present human and material resources of Mauritania. In view of the acute shortage of cadres, and more specifically of high-level cadres, which affects Mauritania (as well as many other African countries), it seemed desirable to select staff of medium level with several years' fieldwork experience in order to ensure a personnel 'representative' of national resources.

(ii) The specific tasks in the project require that the staff have the following qualifications (over and above their own training): a clear understanding and acceptance of the objectives of the project; a knowledge of traditional systems of production and agricultural practices; familiarity with alternative tools and methods and an appreciation of their impact on the overall system of production; the ability to speak the local language and experience of life in the area; pedagogical and administrative competence.

Shortly after the agreement with the Government was signed the staff was selected, and is at present working on the initial stage of the project with the help of an expatriate agricultural engineer (J. Torrealba).

148

THE SUPPORT AND EVALUATION TEAM

As mentioned above, the team acts as the representative of War on Want responsible to the governmental authorities, and is engaged in a number of tasks connected with the project:

— first, to provide assistance to the village representatives and the project staff in formulating annual plans;
— secondly, to supervise the progress of the project and its administration as carried out by the staff;
— finally, to further the research work undertaken during the initial diagnosis and to offer regular support in the evaluation of current activities.

The team comprises the original researchers (Claude Raynaut, Phillip Bradley, Jorge Torrealba), Christopher Robbins and Richard Elsner (War on Want).

Characteristic *Acacia nilotica* woodland in an undisturbed area of *walo* at Lobali. (March 1975.)

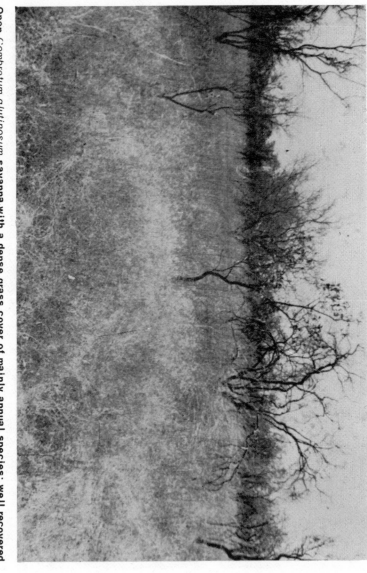

Open *Combretum glutinosum* savanna with a dense grass cover of mainly annual species; well recovered after the 1968-73 drought. (March 1975.)

Panoramic view of typical open savanna south of Gabou. The typical tree is *Combretum glutinosum,* **with occasional specimins of** *Adamsonia digitata* **(right centre) and** *Sterculia setigera.* **(February 1975.)**

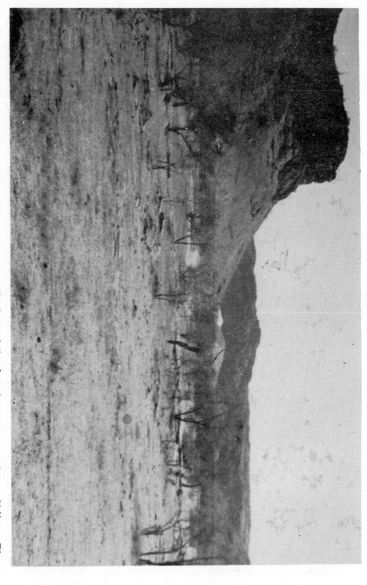

Poor quality *Balanites aegyptiaca* shrub savanna at the foot of the Assaba escarpment near Ndieo. The area is heavily grazed by goats. (March 1975.)

Evidence of environmental deterioration on the *fonde* near Gouraye. Notable features are heavily cut *Balanites aegyptiaca* (for domestic fuel) and surface capping of the predominantly silty soil. (February 1975.)

Evidence of gulley erosion on the *fonde* north of Diaguili. Rows of freshly planted seed scrapes are observable on the right. (July 1 976.)

Cattle pens at Diaguili. The contrast between the dark staining of the manured soils inside the pen, and the lighter non-manured soils outside is noticeable. Behind the pen is the Bondampu Collengal. (July 1976.)

Aerial view of the Senegal valley alluvium. In the foreground are the village lands of Koughani (Senegal) and on the opposite bank is Diaguili (Mauritania). The principal alluvial zones of the valley can be seen: the flooded *walo* with *Acacia nilotica* (1); *fonde* with fields (2); similar cultivated *fonde* (3); and flooded *walo* (4) in Mauritania. The drier *dieri* can be seen in the distance (5). (August 1975.)

Walo north of Koughani, showing dense *Acacia nilotica* (1) woodland, cleared ground and a fenced agricultural area (2) and typical *dieri* trees on the hill in the foreground (3). February 1975.

Storage huts and corrugated iron roofs in Diaguili. The village is situated on the high *fonde*. A small drainage channel separates this from the overgrazed, lower *fonde* in the foreground. (July 1976.)

The village of Ndieo, in the far north of the Guidimaka at the foot of the Assaba escarpment. The photograph shows the cohesion of the village, the lack of herbaceous vegetation on the surrounding land and the dark staining of the soil in the cattle pens in the foreground.

Freshly dug area of *rakhe* east of Moulessinou. *Acacia seyal* (1) and *Mitragyna inermis* (2) in the background. (July 1976.)

Newly planted *Katamagne* east of Moulessimou. Several sorghum seeds are sown in each scrape. The distance between seed holes is approximately one metre. Stalks from the previous years crop are visible. (July 1 976.)

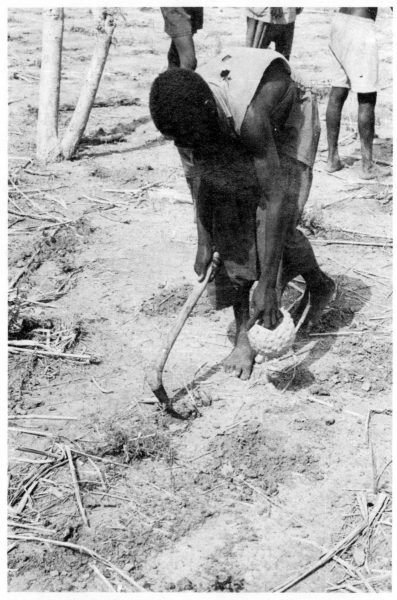

Sowing of sorghum seed on the *rakhe* south east of Diaguili. A small
hole is dug with the tool in the right hand. Several seeds are dropped in
from the small calabash in the left hand and the hole is firmed down with
the feet as the farmer progresses across the field. (July 1 976.)

A heavy digging tool, used for preparing fresh ground. (July 1976.)

The *sakade*, a light digging hoe used for preparing seed holes. (July 1 976.)

The small calabash used as a seed container, and from which seeds are dropped using the thumb and forefinger. (July 1 976.)

Where fields are distant from the village shelters are constructed and the farmers may spend several days at work without returning to the village. Such shelters are particularly necessary when the ripening crops have to be constantly guarded.

The crop (in this case sorghum) is bent over to assist drying immediately prior to the harvest.

Communal threshing of the sorghum harvest.

Construction of a fence to protect the as yet unprepared village garden. This represents the first initiative of the village associations.

Taking the heads of grain to the village. The donkey is the principal means of transport.

Clearing the plot and preparing the collective work force is inspired by the piper on the left.

Bibliography

Actuel Developpement, Sept., Oct. 1974, 'La Politique des grands barrages hydro-agricoles', pp.32-37.

Adam, J.G., 1968, 'Conservation of Vegetation in Africa South of the Sahara', *Acta Phytogeographica Suecica*, no. 54, Uppsala.

Ahn, P.M., 1970, *West African Soils*, Oxford University Press.

Anderson, B., 1957, *A Survey of Soils in the Kongwa and Nachingwea Districts of Tanganyika*, University of Reading.

Annales des Services Meteorologiques de la France d'Outre-Mer, Météorologie Nationale Française.

Archives Pluviometriques du Service Meteorologique du Senegal, A.S.E.C.N.A.

Bathily, A., 1969, 'Notes socio-historiques sur l'ancien royaume Soninke du Gadiaga', *Bulletin de l'IFAN*, Tome XXXI, Série B.

_____, 1972, 'La conquête française du Haut-Fleuve (Sénégal) 1818-1887', *Bulletin de l'IFAN*, Tome XXXIV, Série B. no. 1.

Bergues, H., 1973, 'L'immigration des travailleurs africains noirs en France et particulièrement dans la région parisienne', *Population* no. 1, Janvier-Février, pp.59-80.

Berhault, J., 1967, *Flore du Sénégal*, Edition Clairafrique, Dakar.

Boutillier, J.L. and Cantrelle, P., *et al.*, 1962, *La moyenne vallée du Sénégal — etude socio-economique*, P.U.F.

Bowen, I.S., 1926, 'The ratio of heat losses by conduction and by evaporation from any water surface', *Phys. Rev.* series 2, no. 27, pp.779-87.

Bradley, P.N., 1973, 'The delayed start to the 1973 rains at Samaru, Nigeria', *Savanna* no. 2, pp.78-81.

Brasseur, G., 1968, *Les établissements humains au Mali*, I.F.A.N., Dakar.

Bureau International du Travail (I.L.O.), 1974, *Recherches rétrospectives sur les problemes de la migration*, Geneva.

Connaissance du Senegal, 1965, 'Climats régionaux', *Etudes Sénégalaises* no. 9, fascicule 3, Saint-Louis.

Codjo, Medegan, 1972, 'Régionalisation et Développement. Analyse critique des documents concernant l'aménagement hydro-agricole des grandes vallées d'Afrique Occidentale francophone', Research Paper, l'Université de Bordeaux III.

Daniel, F., 1910, 'Etude sur les Soninkes ou Sarakoles', *Anthropologie*.

Delwaulle, J.C., 1973, 'Résultats de six ans d'observations sur l'érosion au Niger', *Bois et Forêts des Tropiques* no. 150, pp.15-35.

Depierre, D. and Gillet, H., 1971, 'Desertification de la zone sahélienne au Tchad', *Bois et Forêts des Tropiques* no. 139, pp.3-25.

D'Hoore, J.L., 1964, *Soil Map of Africa, scale 1 to 5,000,000*, Explanatory Monograph, Lagos.

Dia, Moukari, 1965, 'L'histoire et les faits', *Faim et Soif* no. 61.

Diarra, S., 1964, 'Les travailleurs africains noirs en France', Thèse de doctorat de 3éme Cycle de Géographie, Université de Paris.

Dubresson, mars 1974, 'Les travailleurs Soninké et Toucouleur dans l'ouest parisien', mimeo.

150

Dussauze-Ingrand, 'Effets de l'immigration sur la région de départ', I.D.E.P./ET/R/24.16.

Garnier, B.J., 1967, *Weather Conditions in Nigeria*, McGill University, Climatological Research, series 2.

Greenberg, J.H., 1946, 'The influence of Islam on a Sudanese religion', *Monograph of the American Ethogical Society*, New York, pp.12-26.

Halwagy, R., 1962, 'The incidence of the biotic factor in northern Sudan', *Oikos* no. 13, pp.97-117.

Institut Africain de Developpement Economique et de Planification (IDEP), 1972, 'Les aspects de l'immigration des travailleurs d'Afrique noire et leurs rapports avec la condition clandestine', I.D.E.P. ET/25.14.

Kane, A.S., 1935, 'Du régime des terres chez les populations du Fouta Sénégalais', *Bulletin Comité Etudes historiques et scientifiques de l'A.O.F.*, XVIII, pp.449-61.

Kane, F. and Lericollais, A., 1974, 'L'émigration en pays Soninke', mimeo, Dakar.

Kowal, J., 1970, 'Effect of an exceptional storm on soil conservation at Samaru, Nigeria', *Nigerian Geography J.*, no. 13, pp.163-74.

Le Blanc, C., 1962, 'Etude humaine de deux villages de Damga', Mémoire de Géographie, Faculté des Lettres et Sciences Humaines, Bordeaux.

M'Bow, 1974, 'Plus de ghetto culturel pour les "migrants" en France', *Eurafrique*, no. 250, pp.2-5.

Merlin, P. and Cheret, I., n.d., 'La Politique de l'Eau', Rapport à la Direction Générale des Travaux Publics, *Gouvernement Géneral de l'A.O.F., Service de l'hydraulique 'La Vallée du Sénégal'*.

Michel, P., 1965, 'Recherches pédologiques au Sénégal et en Mauritanie Méridionale', *Revue de Géographie de l'Afrique occidentale*, no. 1.2, pp.169-85.

———, 1973, *Les Bassins des Fleuves Sénégal et Gambie, Etude géomorphologique*, 3 vols., O.R.S,T.O.M., Paris.

Ministere d'Outre-Mer, *Le Fleuve, 2 ème partie: Analyse de la sous-zone Sarakolé: Etude socio-économique*.

Mission d'Amenagement du Fleuve Senegal, 1960, *La Vallée du Fleuve*, Tome II, présentation (CHERET, I.), Bureau: Centre Et. Equipem. Outremer., Paris, mimeo.

———, 1962, *Les Sols de la Région de Matalu*, (MAYNARD, J.), Société Générale des Travaux Hydro-Agricoles, 2 vols.

———, 1966, *Monographie Hydrologique du Fleuve Sénégal, Partie 4, Recueil de Données Numériques, Tome 5, Débits Journaliers dans le Vallée*, ROCHETTE, C., O.R.S.T.O.M., Dakar.

Mortimore, M.J. and Wilson, J., 1965, 'Land and people in the Kano close-settled zone', Ahmadu Bello University, Dept. Geogr. Occ., Paper no. 1.

O.R.S.T.O.M., 1951, *Cartes de l'élevage pour la Mauritanie*, Paris.

Papy, L., 1951, 'La vallée du Sénégal', *Cahiers d'Outre-mer*, no. 16, pp.1-48 (Agriculture traditionelle et riziculture mécanisée), Bordeaux.

Penman, H.L., 1948, 'Natural evaporation from open water, bare soil and grass', *Proc. Roy. Soc.*, no. 193, London, pp.120-45.

Pollet, E. and Winter, G., 1968, 'L'organisation sociale du travail agricole des Soninkés (Dyahuna, Mali)', *Cahiers d'Etudes Africaines*, vol. VIII, no. 32, 4ème Cahier, pp.509-34, Paris.

———, 1971, *La Société Soninké (Dyahunu, Mali)*, Université de Bruxelles, Ed. de l'Institut de Sociologie.

Poupon, H. and Bille, J.C., 1974, 'Recherches écologiques sur une savane sáhélienne du Ferlo septentrional, Sénégal: Influence de la sécheresse de l'année 1972-1973 sur la strate ligneuse', *La Terre et la Vie* no. 28, pp.49-75.

Ravault, F., 1964, 'Kanel: l'exode rural dans un village de la vallée du Sénégal', *Cahiers d'Outre-Mer*, vol. 16, no. 65, Bordeaux.

Raynaut, C., 1973, *Structures normatives et relations électives*, Mouton.

———, 1977, 'Circulation monétaire et évolution des structures socio-économiques chez les Haoussas du Niger', *Africa*, no. 2, London.

Rochette, G. and Toucheboeuf, P., 1964, 'Aperçu hydrologique du Fleuve Sénégal: Synthèse provisoire des données hydrologiques', Rapport au Ministère d'Outre-mer, O.R.S.T.O.M.

Saint Pere, J.H., 1925, *Les Sarakollé du Guidimaka*, Comité d'etudes historiques et scientifiques de l'Afrique Occidentale Francaise, Paris.

Seck, A., 1965, 'Les escales du Fleuve Sénégal', *Revue de Géographie de l'Afrique Occidentale*, no. 1-2, pp.71-118.

Service de l'Hydraulique de l'Afrique Occidentale Française, various, *Fleuve Sénégal, Releves des Echelles limnimetriques*, Paris.

Thornthwaite, C.W. and Mather, J.R., 1955, 'The water balance', *Drexel Institute of Technology, Labs. Climatology*, no. 8 (1), pp.22-67.

———, 1957, 'Instructions and Tables for computing Potential Evapo-transpiration and the Water Balance', *Climatology* no. 10 (3), Laboratory of Climatology, Centerton, New Jersey.

Trochain, J., 1940, 'Contribution à l'étude de la végétation du Sénégal', *Mem. Inst. Fr. Afr. Noire*, no. 2, Paris.

Union Generale des Travailleurs Senegalais en France, 1970, *Le livre des travailleurs africains en France*, Cahiers libres, F. Maspero.

Wilde, J. de, 1971, 'Le Développement agricole en Afrique tropicale. Problèmes de main-d'oeuvre et d'emploi', I.L.O. vol. 104, no. 5, pp.403-22.

Glossaries

TERMS DENOTING TOPOGRAPHIC FORM

terminology	language	description and alternative names
falo	T/S	upper segment of bank
wuso	S	lower segment of bank
fonde	T/S	levee
fonde ranere	T/S	upper segment of levee (*fonde blanc*)
fonde wallere	T/S	lower segment of levee (*fonde ballere fonde wallere fonde noir*)
fare	S	raised area on *fonde* or sand bar in river
napo	S	small depression in *fonde*
diacre	T	a stepped series of minor levees usually on the inside of meanders
walo	T/S	sedimentary basin behind levee
hollalde ranere	T	upper segment of *walo* (*hollalde blanc*)
hollalde wallere	T	lower segment of *walo* (*hollalde ballere hollalde wallere hollalde noir*)
vendou	T	permanent or semi-permanent lakes in the bottom of large basins or in major depressions
khare	S	between the levees of the *fonde*
djedjogol	T	marginal colluvium and alluvium of the Senegal valley
dieri	T/S	general term for non-alluvial areas
guillu	S	long sand ridge in the *dieri*
rakhe	S	alluvial depressions of interior tributaries
paraole	S	marginal slopes and plains of interior drainage systems

TERMS DENOTING SOIL TYPE

terminology	language	descriptions and alternative names
collengal	T/S	an area of *walo* used for agriculture
katamagne	S	clay-rich soil found in the *rakhe*
niarwalle	S	soil containing less clay than the *katamagne*, usually associated with the *paraole*, but also found in pediplains
niarikata	S	clay-enriched soil within the *niarwalle*
signa bine	S	darker and lighter coloured sandy soils of
signa khole	S	the *dieri* .
signa kape	S	colluvial material overlying alluvium where valley meets the *dieri*. Generally less sandy than other types of *signa*.

Areas of these soils or topographic units may be further specified by prefixes denoting location:

Budampu collengal, worokhomo signa, khirin kare

SOCIOLOGICAL TERMS (SONINKE)

nyinyagumme	— controller of land
nyinyantiekhe	— payment in kind to *nyinyagumme* for the use of land
muso	— leasing of land
ka	— large family unit
kagumme	— family head
tekhore	— the land holdings of the *ka*
salluma	— land to which the family have collective rights of use, but which is cultivated by individual males of the family
yakharinte	— land to which the family have collective rights of use, but which is cultivated by individual women of the family
duntegne	— a 'man of confidence' who looks after and invests funds derived from the remittances of migrant working overseas
dundukhuma	— the personal savings of an emigrant worker
tama	— an engagement present
futte	— a dowry given to a woman on marriage
nabure	— a gift for the male relative of the bride

TERMS DENOTING CROP VARIETIES (SONINKE)

sorghum (*fella*) (loose panicle)	*mangagne badiabale* *fella* *nabane leme*
sorghum (*nienico*) (dense panicle)	*khore* *maundo* *sidi nieliba* *sile tombe* *sile maya* *samba dieri*
millet (Pennisetum)	*suna* *sagno*
cowpeas	*niebe*
maize	*dumbe*
groundnut	*tiga sasa* *tiga fune*
rice	*maro sinisire* *maro kas barene* *maro khore*

PLACE NAMES CITED IN THE TEXT

riverine settlements in the Guidimaka	riverine settlements in neighbouring areas of Senegal
Betselba	Bakel
Diogountourou	Ballou
Diaguili	Diawara
Gouraye	Golmi
Khabou	Kounghani
Lexelba	Lobali
Moulessimou	Manael
Sangue-Dieri	Mouderi
Solou	Tuabou
Takoutala	Yelingara
Woumpou	

other settlements in the Guidimaka	other settlements in neighbouring areas of Senegal
Agouemit	Fadiara
Ajar-Sarakole	Gabou
Artemou	Gounia
Baediam	Tourime
Bokedianbi	Ololdou

	settlements in surrounding regions
Bouanze	
Bouly	
Dafort	Fete Ole (Senegal)
Harr	Kaedi
Hassi-Chaggar	Kayes (Mali)
Mbedia-Achar	Kidira (Senegal)
Ndieo	Kiffa
Ould Yenze	Maghama
Oulombome	Matam (Senegal)
Saboussine	Mbout
Selibabi	Podor (Senegal)

	tributaries of the Senegal river
Soufi	
Testai	Faleme
Yeli-Male	Garfa
	Karakoro
	Niorde

Selected Rainfall and Evaporation Statistics for the Middle Senegal Valley

ANNUAL RAINFALL TOTALS FOR SELIBABI, KIDIRA, BAKEL AND MATAM 1922-75

Year	Selibabi	Kidira	Bakel	Matam
1922			517	640
1923			514	492
1924			546	406
1925			496	557
1926			305	334
1927			532	703
1928			557	453
1929			—	—
1930			552	646
1931		584	447	—
1932		—	411	—
1933	589	1273	536	640
1934	675	941	525	746
1935	—	464	464	658
1936	1100	—	656	1242
1937	527	1135	564	551
1938	624	678	531	538
1939	—	—	427	475
1940	577	1099	501	563
1941	428	678	525	255
1942	350	717	375	516
1943	705	739	407	456
1944	365	510	345	296
1945	711	953	587	419
1946	672	681	611	550
1947	823	628	553	380
1948	558	675	575	414
1949	614	650	607	389
1950	—	962	632	714
1951	653	1012	467	681
1952	728	680	458	603
1953	790	815	427	471

ANNUAL TOTAL RAINFALLS (Cont.)

Year	Selibabi	Kidira	Bakel	Matam
1954	579	663	357	482
1955	722	851	513	477
1956	565	–	595	585
1957	–	–	489	453
1958	564	–	235	690
1959	613	874	689	538
1960	–		–	486
1961	643		366	480
1962	613		317	445
1963	533		528	486
1964	610		469	507
1965	955		751	701
1966	560		700	522
1967	810		900	329
1968	414		484	286
1969	510	762	575	534
1970	388	598	457	281
1971	554	552	541	431
1972	606	623	369	175
1973	444	410	396	220

MONTHLY RAINFALL, PROBABILITIES AND EVAPORATION ESTIMATES FOR BAKEL

(1) *Average monthly rainfall (mm.), May to October*

	M	J	J	A	S	O	total
mean monthly rainfall (1922-73)	6	48	118	181	116	28	497

(ii) *Probability estimates (rainfall may be equal to, or below the following levels)*

number of years in ten	M	J	J	A	S	O
1	0	15	44	92	44	1
2	0	18	68	117	55	5
3	0	32	84	139	67	8
4	0	36	91	147	90	14
5	1	40	102	161	107	20
6	2	45	130	185	118	23
7	3	56	150	205	129	34
8	8	66	164	240	159	45
9	16	83	190	295	215	59

(iii) *Potential evaporation (mm.)*

a.	184	159	138	122	127	146
b.	216	178	144	118	124	139
c.	426	385	266	283	231	256
d.	413	345	215	121	121	172

a. mean of 12 Sahelian stations of similar latitude (open water)
b. mean over 10 years from Kayes (open water)
c. calculated for Matam using Thornthwaite's (*1955*) formula based on temperature
d. mean over 10 years from Matam (open water)

Variation in Rainfall between Two Recording Stations at Bakel (1955-65) (mm.)

Rainfall (mm.) May-October	MAS station (river)	ASECNA station (airfield)	% difference
1955	782.3	512.9	−34.4
1956	608.0	595.1	− 2.1
1957	700.2	488.5	−30.2
1958	441.2	234.6	−46.8
1959	561.6	688.8	+22.6
1960*	586.6	395.4	−32.6
1961	645.2	365.5	−43.3
1962	531.3	307.0	−42.2
1963**	336.3	423.1	+25.8
1964	480.6	468.7	− 2.5
1965	760.5	748.6	− 1.6

*excluding September
**excluding September and October

The Duration of Active Flooding of the Senegal River at Bakel (1904-64)

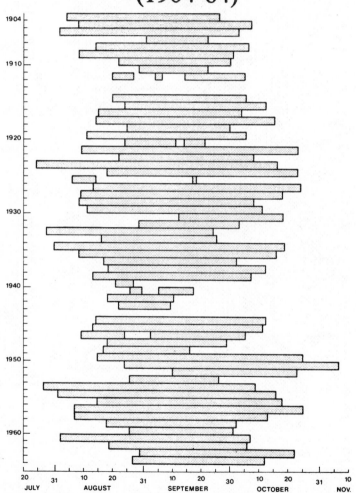

Active flooding is assumed to commence when discharge exceeds 2000 cubic metres per second, and is portrayed by the dark bar.

The Geology of the Guidimaka and the Bakel Region

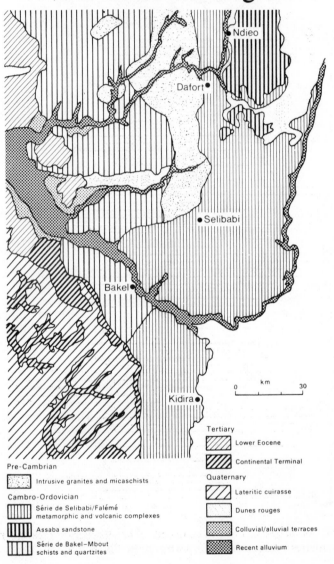

Ndieo

Dafort

Selibabi

Bakel

km
0   30

Kidira

Tertiary

Lower Eocene

Continental Terminal

Pre-Cambrian

Intrusive granites and micaschists

Cambro-Ordovician

Série de Selibabi/Falémé
metamorphic and volcanic complexes

Assaba sandstone

Série de Bakel–Mbout
schists and quartzites

Quaternary

Lateritic cuirasse

Dunes rouges

Colluvial/alluvial terraces

Recent alluvium

The Geomorphological Evolution of the Senegal River Alluvium and its Relationship to the Soils

The solid geology, which is largely responsible for the variations in soil type and quality in the *dieri*, is obscured by a thick mantle of alluvial deposits throughout the Senegal valley itself. Broadly speaking, this alluvium falls into two major types: sand-rich deposits forming levees and terraces, and the clay sediments which are found in depressions. This coarse division obscures a more complex subset of landforms which themselves have individual qualities of importance to soil status, vegetation, and agriculture. The differences between these various sub-types is best understood in terms of their historical evolution.

The first deposits of immediate interest were those formed at the margins of the valley during the Ogolien phase (contemporaneous with the recent Wurm of Europe). These are both alluvial and colluvial, termed *le premier remblai*, and were deposited during a long dry period, when the Senegal river was incapable of carrying a heavy sediment load. Mixed material (mainly sand) was deposited along the margins of the valley. This material is variable in composition, though generally sandy rather than clayey. It is generally included within the Toucouleur name *djedjogol*, and may be synonymous with *signa kape* in the Guidimaka.

During this arid phase, a series of dunes was formed throughout northern Senegal and southern Mauritania (the *dunes rouges*). The dunes progressed southwards down the Atlantic coast, west of Rosso, thereby cutting off the mouth of the Senegal river. As the climate became wetter following the Ogolien, the river proceeded to recut its bed into the deposits laid down during the arid phase. The increased humidity was responsible for the initiation of iron mobilisation in the *premier remblai*. This period culminated in a marine transgression taking place in the region of 11000 to 8000 BP, and in which more progressive ferruginisation of the soils took place.

Between 7500 and 5500 BP, the climate again became drier and a *deuxieme remblai* was formed, with characteristics similar to the first. Both these deposits are found in the middle valley, and rest at the level attained by the annual flood.

Subsequent to this earlier development, we enter the recent Quaternary, in which the most important developments within the valley have taken place. This latter period commenced with a second marine transgression termed the 'Nouakchottian', accompanied by an increasingly humid climate. From this period on a complex system of levees, minor channels, and sedimentary basins was formed within the valley itself. The Nouakchottian raised the base level of the river and initiated the deposition of sediments to form the *hautes levées*. The sediments are usually composed of fine sand and silt. Smaller, *petites levées*, formed during the same period, have often been breached by flood waters which penetrate the basins (*cuvettes*) lying between the *hautes levées* and the *premier remblai*. The *petites levées* are formed along minor channels crossing these basins. The rupturing of these small levees has led to the formation of small deltas within the *cuvettes*. These are termed *deltas de rupture de levée*. All these deposits are sandy in nature though less homogeneous than the high levees. The development of these features continued from 5000 to 2000 BP, indicating a flow regime with significantly greater run-off and load-carrying capacity than today. The present climate is less humid than this post-Nouakchottian phase. The levees formed during this wet phase constitute the *fonde*. Towards the end of this period the Senegal river itself began to form and occupy the meander system which is at present in evidence.

A third, minor dry phase followed, in which the height of the flood, and the competence of the river, were insufficient to sustain the continued formation of the high levees or the deltas resulting from their rupture. Instead, a series of smaller levees (*subactuelles*) were formed, usually inside large meanders and behind the high levees, their altitude decreasing steadily up to the present. Between these smaller levees, minor depressions (*lits mineurs*) collect finer sediments deposited during the annual flood. Where the levees border the main channel they are given the Toucouleur name of *diacre*. The progressive migration downstream of the meanders, especially at the present time, has led to re-erosion of many of these smaller levee systems. A final term, *levées actuelles*, is given to those which, at the present time, form the high banks of the Senegal river.

The geomorphological terminology described above is matched by local names,[1] whose function is more a description of agricultural potential — emphasising the relationship between geomorphology, hydrology and soils. The *djedjogol, fonde* and *diacre* have already been mentioned. The large sediment basins are termed the *walo,* itself divided into *vendou* (small permanent lakes at the bottom of the basins), *hollalde noir* (*hollalde wallere*) (lower slopes) and *hollalde* (*hollalde ranere*) (upper margins). The *fonde,* like the *walo,* is divided into *fonde noir* (*fonde ballere*) and *fonde blanc* (*fonde ranere*), again signifying lower and upper components respectively. Where tortuous drainage channels meander across the *walo* their *petites levées* and 'deltas' give rise to good soils reserved for maize. These are termed *walo-wallere* or *fonde wallere.* They are usually found on the margins of the *hollalde wallere,* with clay-rich, though uncompacted soils. Finally, we may specify the *falo* as the river banks of the high levees.

The development of soils within these landforms is related to age, elevation and hydrology. Broadly speaking, those of the basins are older, more clay-rich and hydromorphic, whilst those of the levees contain more sand and silt, are less hydromorphic, and sometimes poorly developed. A more detailed description is as follows:

1.   The lowest parts of the basins may contain permanent lakes. The soils of these *vendou* areas are dominated by clay (50% +), are in a condition of permanent reduction due to submergence in excess of 150 days. They are now termed *sols à gley.*

2.   In the *walo* areas submerged from 30 to 120 days, soils are still clay-rich (30-50%), also hydromorphic, but more pseudogleyed than gleyed (re-oxidation evident during dry season), especially as the submersion period is reduced. They are termed *vertisols* or *para-vertisols topomorphes,* though formerly *sols tirs sur argile de decantation.* They fall within the group *sols hydromorphes peu humifères a pseudogley,* sub-group *sols à taches et concrétions.* As the name suggests, they are characterised by the presence firstly, of mottles, and secondly, of concretions.

3.   The soils of the older levees, and especially their lower zones (*fonde ballere* or *fonde noir*) and of the 'deltas' are again classified as *sols a pseudogley,* though in this case note vertisolic because of the decrease of clay (20-30%) and increase in silt (15-25%) and sand (50-70%).

4.   The *fonde ranere* (*fonde blanc*) soils are more difficult to define. Where they are derived from the high levees, *sols hydromorphes a pseudogley* may exist, though the mottling will occur at depth, but where levees are more recent or drier, *sols peu evolués d'apport* either 'modal' or *hydromorphe,* may occur. Their principal characteristic is an increase in sand content (60-85%) and a commensurate decrease in silt (5-20%). These *fonde ranere* areas

are more frequently used for agriculture than the *fonde ballere* because they are always above the maximum flood level, and are therefore suitable for rainy-season cultivation like the *dieri*.
5. Finally, we may distinguish the *djedjogol* areas, where soil is characteristically a *sol à pseudogley*, with the usual mottles and concretions. The relative proportions of sand, silt and clay in these soils are highly variable, and insufficient samples were collected to enable a satisfactory characterisation to be attempted. Flooding may vary from 0 to 30 days.

NOTE

1 These are Toucouleur names, and are applied throughout the Senegal valley, particularly in the lower reaches. The Soninke of the Guidimaka incorporate elements of this terminology, but only as an adjunct to their own system.

APPENDIX F

Soil Analyses

Analyses, both chemical and physical, were completed on 53 soil samples. These were collected over the complete range of terrain types specified above and give a comprehensive indication, both of the contrasts between these terrain types, and within the units themselves. They are arranged in two major, and several minor sub-groups:

    (i)   Alluvial soils
         A1 *Fonde blanc (fonde ranere)*
         A2 *Fonde noir (fonde wallere)*
         A3 *Hollalde blanc*
         A4 *Hollalde noir*
         A5 *Vendou*
         A6 *Djedjogol*

    (ii) *Dieri* soils
         B1 Lateritic
         B2 Hillslopes within the alluvial lands
         B3 *Dune rouge*
         B4 Banks of interior marigots
         B5 Others

Alluvial soils

A1   High *fonde* soils from locations between Lobali and Ballou in Senegal. High pH is as expected, mediocre CEC, very variable P (though generally good). Fluctuations in organic matter are largely due to the condition of the vegetation. Thus 1 and 30 are badly degraded, whereas 16 supports well-developed bush.

A2   Low *fonde* soils showing mottling at depth (hydromorphic), have lower pH, slightly higher CEC. Other characteristics are similar except for a substantial increase in clay content. B1 is interesting for its high pH and Na; a localised rather than general condition.

A3   High *walo* areas with greater hydromorphic development and increasing clay content. They are regularly flooded and thus have lower pH. These soils should be more fertile than A2, although figures suggest similar CEC and lower P. This is due to the fact that these soils are from cultivated land (except 10 and 11) and have therefore lost P and organic matter. The contrast between 10 and 11 and the others indicates the effects of cultivation (loss of P and organic matter). The lower values for Mg and Ca (and therefore CEC) of 10 and 11 may result from their position at the interior edge of the *walo*, the others being from the riverside — near the villages, hence cultivation.

A4   Low *walo* areas, flooded annually, with high clay percentages. Distinctive features are low pH, high CEC — increasing towards the lowest areas (33 and 34), and generally high P and organic matter. The high value for Na for soil 8 may cause problems for agriculture. The contrast between 34 and Y4/K2 is interesting. The former is from natural *Acacia nilotica* forest north of Lobali. With no evidence of degradation through human activity (except for spasmodic goat grazing of seeds), this represents the optimum of soil-vegetation quality in the alluvial lands. Notable chemical properties are high CEC (particularly K), high P and high organic matter. 53, from dense (again undisturbed) *Acacia nilotica* forest south of Ndieo, is similar, and indicates that the smaller alluvial systems of interior Mauritania can be productive. Y4 and K2 are from similar topographic positions, but are or have been recently cultivated. The lower

CEC, K. P and organic matter demonstrate the effects of agriculture, suggesting that, despite annual replenishment through flooding, soil depletion may in fact occur in the *walo* lands. 12 and R1 show much higher pH and in the field were deeply cracked, suggesting vertisolic development.

A5　The lowest parts of the *walo* support permanent lakes throughout the dry season. They are sequential extensions of A4, with similar properties to 33 and 34. Though fertile, they are flooded for long periods and are waterlogged throughout the year. Without drainage, which might well destroy their fertility, they are unsuitable and inaccessible for cultivation.

A6　Two soils from the margins of the *walo* and the *dieri* are sandier than neighbouring *walo* soils, developed in colluvium, and show different chemical properties: high pH, CEC, K, mediocre P, and high organic matter.

These alluvial soils are generally fertile, though K levels less than 0.3 indicate potential deficiency, especially for long-period crops such as sorghum. P levels are generally high (2 to 4 being normal for the wetter savanna lands to the south). The analyses represent the chemical condition of the soils during the dry season. During the rains, and the cultivation season, their characteristics may well alter. In many cases I suspect the high cation and P levels are due to upward capillary movement, particularly in the clay soils. Such capillary enrichment of the surface horizon is unlikely to be so strong during the wet season.

Analysis of soils taken from alluvial lands of Senegal valley

		pH	CEC	Na	K	Mg	Ca	P	N	C	% sand	% silt	% clay
A1	1.	7.0	8.0	0.0	0.7	2.4	6.5	119.4	0.08	0.66	83.5	7.0	9.5
	30.	6.4	4.2	0.0	0.3	1.3	3.0	14.0	0.05	0.76	82.5	10.0	7.5
	K1.	5.7	9.2	0.0	0.3	2.7	5.5	21.7	0.08	1.11	62.5	20.0	17.5
	16.	7.0	10.5	0.0	0.4	2.1	9.8	73.7	0.12	1.68	76.5	15.0	8.5
	20.	6.6	11.1	0.0	0.5	2.0	9.8	180.6	0.09	1.37	67.5	18.0	14.5
	32.	5.1	4.6	0.0	0.2	1.3	2.4	22.8	0.06	0.98	86.5	4.5	9.0
A2	2.	5.9	7.7	0.1	0.2	2.4	4.6	10.2	0.06	0.72	64.5	17.0	18.5
	3.	5.9	8.2	0.1	0.3	2.5	4.8	12.9	0.06	0.72	62.5	15.0	22.5
	4.	5.7	18.0	0.1	0.3	4.6	8.8	9.6	0.20	2.33	56.5	18.0	25.5
	13.	5.5	10.2	0.0	0.2	2.9	5.8	6.5	0.06	1.35	62.5	5.0	32.5
	15.	5.4	15.4	0.0	0.4	4.1	7.2	72.2	0.12	1.64	51.5	25.0	23.5
	35.	5.9	18.5	0.1	0.6	6.2	9.8	20.3	0.08	1.03	46.0	20.0	34.0
	Y1.	5.4	14.6	0.4	0.2	3.8	6.5	7.7	0.04	1.00	44.5	20.0	35.5
	R5.	5.4	20.8	0.1	0.3	6.2	9.5	6.3	0.08	0.96	26.5	29.0	44.5
	B1.	8.3	14.4	4.6	0.1	2.8	10.0	22.1	0.04	0.49	41.5	30.0	28.5
A3	10.	5.5	9.2	0.1	0.3	1.2	5.0	13.6	0.15	2.12	74.5	14.0	11.5
	11.	5.0	10.8	0.0	0.3	2.3	4.0	15.8	0.13	1.86	64.5	17.0	18.5
	R4.	4.9	17.2	0.3	0.2	4.3	6.9	7.2	0.06	0.73	30.0	28.5	41.5
	R3.	5.7	20.5	0.1	0.2	6.4	11.7	8.5	0.05	0.96	26.5	51.0	22.5
	R2.	5.2	18.4	0.3	0.3	6.2	7.8	6.3	0.07	0.79	17.5	55.0	27.5
	Y2.	4.9	13.9	0.3	0.2	3.6	6.0	7.3	0.06	0.59	41.0	23.5	35.5
	Y3.	4.7	14.6	0.2	0.2	3.3	5.3	7.4	0.06	0.97	53.0	23.0	24.0

Analysis of soils taken from alluvial lands of Senegal valley (cont.)

		pH	CEC	Na	K	Mg	Ca	P	N	C	% sand	% silt	% clay
A4	R1.	6.3	27.4	0.3	0.5	11.5	14.3	11.1	0.05	0.84	14.5	53.0	35.5
	8.	4.7	17.4	0.8	0.5	2.5	6.8	78.9	0.24	3.28	58.5	19.0	22.5
	B2.	4.8	18.4	0.4	0.4	4.7	7.3	11.1	0.18	2.27	35.5	21.0	43.5
	Y4.	4.7	14.5	0.2	0.3	3.0	4.8	9.2	0.08	0.74	43.0	23.5	33.5
	K2.	4.6	17.3	0.2	0.3	3.3	6.2	13.9	0.11	1.68	41.5	24.0	34.5
	33.	4.5	31.9	0.1	0.6	8.1	13.0	40.3	0.20	2.38	43.5	18.0	38.5
	34.	4.4	42.8	0.3	1.2	7.2	16.5	62.6	0.44	4.70	51.5	15.5	33.0
	12.	5.1	15.9	0.1	0.4	3.7	6.0	24.3	0.17	2.21	63.5	8.0	28.5
	53.	4.9	21.1	0.4	1.1	5.2	6.9	66.3	0.20	2.40	44.5	10.5	45.0
A5	6.	4.9	35.8	0.2	1.1	5.8	13.2	29.8	0.74	9.70	62.5	14.0	23.5
	7.	4.5	26.0	0.2	1.0	5.2	8.9	46.4	0.21	2.19	34.5	23.0	45.5
A6	17.	6.3	28.0	0.2	0.8	10.8	16.8	12.2	0.11	1.16	29.5	20.0	50.5
	19.	6.7	24.5	0.1	1.0	6.3	15.8	10.9	0.16	2.29	50.5	20.0	29.5

pH – 1:5 H_2O

CEC, Na, K, Mg, Ca – meq/100 gm a.d.s.

P – available p.p.m. NH_4F + HCl

N, C – total N, organic-C o.d.s.

APPENDIX F(ii)

Dieri soils

B1 Soils derived from laterite, either by erosion, or by colluvial transportation. 21 and 24 are from the Continental Terminal south west of Ololdou, 31 beside the piste between Fadiara and Yeli Male, and 54 by the piste 13 km. west of Selibabi, *en route* to Baediam. Notable features are the low CEC, in particular K and Mg.

B2 Undisturbed soils from hillslopes within the alluvial areas; 29 from basalt-derived material and 38 from quartzite.

B3 Both 39 and 52 are from soils developed from the red sands dating from the pre-Nouakchottian arid phase. Poor CEC (as B1) is distinctive.

B4 Banks of interior marigots. 43, 44, and H1 from poorly sorted, coarse material by small channels; 45, 47, 46 and 50 in positions further downstream with finer material. The former three are poor in cations, particularly Mg and Ca. The latter four are slightly more fertile, especially 50, to the west of Ndieo.

B5 Undifferentiated soils from topographic positions which are neither hillslopes nor alluvial depressions. Differences Between the two are based on geology; 41 being derived from Cambro-Ordovician sediments (Série de Selibabi) as is 50 from B4, while 40 has developed in Pre-Cambrian granites and schistes (of similar origin to 43 and 44).

By comparison to the alluvial soils, those from the *dieri* show high pH values though generally lower CEC. As with the alluvium, both P and N, C are very variable and difficult to interpret.

Analysis of soils taken from dieri lands within the Soninke region

		pH	CEC	Na	K	Mg	Ca	P	N	C	% sand	% silt	% clay
B1	21.	5.3	2.4	0.0	0.2	0.3	1.1	20.6	0.07	0.81	83.0	7.5	9.5
	24.	5.5	2.2	0.0	0.1	0.3	1.1	5.5	0.06	1.03	83.5	7.5	9.0
	54.	6.0	5.4	0.1	0.3	1.5	3.4	10.1	0.07	0.93	68.5	17.5	14.0
	31.	6.4	2.2	0.0	0.2	0.5	1.8	8.1	0.04	1.02	88.5	7.5	4.0
B2	29.	6.9	20.6	0.0	0.5	11.8	9.6	9.6	0.26	3.14	74.0	16.0	10.0
	38.	6.2	7.1	0.1	0.3	1.8	6.0	19.2	0.12	2.35	79.0	10.0	11.0
B3	39.	6.6	3.2	0.0	0.2	0.8	3.5	45.7	0.06	0.84	92.5	3.0	4.5
	52.	6.6	2.2	0.0	0.2	0.7	2.3	10.9	0.06	1.21	95.0	2.0	3.0
B5	43.	6.8	5.5	0.0	0.3	1.5	5.3	10.3	0.07	0.73	27.5	38.0	33.5
	44.	6.8	5.2	0.1	0.4	1.5	4.4	15.5	0.08	0.79	82.5	8.0	9.5
	H1.	6.0	3.1	0.0	0.4	0.8	1.8	41.3	0.05	1.20	88.5	3.0	8.5
	45.	6.1	12.3	0.1	0.6	3.6	8.5	33.2	0.10	1.16	61.0	21.5	17.5
	47.	6.6	5.2	0.1	0.4	2.1	4.4	29.5	0.08	1.48	81.0	7.5	11.5
	46.	5.2	8.1	0.0	0.2	2.0	4.9	7.5	0.07	1.66	72.0	10.0	18.0
	50.	6.5	22.7	0.1	0.6	11.7	10.8	17.0	0.07	1.32	48.5	26.0	25.5
B5	41.	6.6	31.5	0.1	0.5	15.5	16.8	13.3	0.08	1.50	54.0	28.0	18.0
	40.	6.4	8.4	0.0	0.4	3.8	5.1	38.3	0.07	1.08	22.5	8.5	14.0